By Fred DeRuvo

SELF

Copyright © 2011 by Study-Grow-Know

All rights reserved. Written permission must be secured from the publisher to use or reproduce any part of this book, except brief quotations in critical reviews or articles.

Published in Scotts Valley, California, by Study-Grow-Know
www.studygrowknow.com • www.rightly-dividing.com

Unless noted, Scripture quotations are from the New American Standard Bible, Copyright ©1960, 1962, 1963, 1968, 1971, 1972, 1973, 1975, 1977, 1995 by The Lockman Foundation.

Cover design by Fred DeRuvo

All images unless otherwise noted were created by Fred DeRuvo

Cover Images by:
© diez-artwork - Fotolia.com, © Yura_fx - Fotolia.com, © Gino Santa Maria - Fotolia.com

Oneplace.com logo on back outside cover is a registered trademark of Oneplace.com and used with permission.

Edited by: Hannah Richards

Library of Congress Cataloging-in-Publication Data

DeRuvo, Fred, 1957 –

ISBN 098370063X
EAN-13 978-0983700630

1. Religion – Christian Life – Personal Growth

Contents

Foreword:		5
Chapter 1:	Self Changes Everything	9
Chapter 2:	Self and Circumcision	18
Chapter 3:	Self and Abortion	24
Chapter 4:	Self and Gay Rights	30
Chapter 5:	Self and Money	39
Chapter 6:	Self and Boasting	46
Chapter 7:	Self and Arrogance	55
Chapter 8:	Self and Reviling	60
Chapter 9:	Self and Disobedience	66
Chapter 10:	Self and Ungratefulness	76
Chapter 11:	Self and Unholiness	83
Chapter 12:	Self in Politics	95
Chapter 13:	Self in Islam	116
Chapter 14:	Self in Legalism	123
Chapter 15:	Self and Truth	133
Chapter 16:	Self and Idolatry	144
Chapter 17:	Self and False Prophets	152
Chapter 18:	Self and False Messiahs	159
Chapter 19:	Self in Society	174
Chapter 20:	Self in Crime	182
Chapter 21:	Self in You	191

"For men will be lovers of self, lovers of money, boastful, arrogant, revilers, disobedient to parents, ungrateful, unholy, unloving, irreconcilable, malicious gossips, without self-control, brutal, haters of good, treacherous, reckless, conceited, lovers of pleasure rather than lovers of God, holding to a form of godliness, although they have denied its power."

– 2 Timothy 3:2-5 (NASB)

FOREWORD

What can we say? Society is failing...*miserably*. Everywhere you look, there are severe signs of wear and tear on the fabric of society to the point that the thin veneer of civility has all but crumbled to dust.

It is likely difficult for many of us to appreciate just exactly *how* much society has changed over the years, because it has not only been a gradual change, but in many ways, an actual overt assault on society that has promoted the change. The one thing I remember that sets my childhood years apart from my adult years is the time that we – as a family – went to a fair. It was in a somewhat large city in California and I could not have been much past 6th or 7th grade.

As we were leaving the fairgrounds toward the parking lot and our car, my sister and I were walking ahead of our parents. Behind us, I could hear my dad and mom talking, and coming up behind them were two tall teenagers, also talking.

As I continued to walk, I heard my father raise his voice just a bit and say something to the two male teens, who by then were walking right near my parents. In the course of the conversation to one another, the two teens used some off-color language that was, at that time, not appropriate for women or children.

I remember seeing my dad's stern expression as he told them (not asked them, mind you) to watch their language around my mom and my sister and me. I recall that without even saying anything, both teens made a beeline for their car, embarrassed with beet red faces. As they walked away, they did not turn back to glare at my father or flip him off. They just kept walking. I was amazed at my dad because of the way he commanded that type of respect.

That was then. If the same situation was transplanted to 2011, there would be a considerably different result. Chances are good that the two male teens would have gotten into a verbal altercation with my father and might have even pumped their fists, or worse, pulled out some type of weapon.

Not only would they have told my father off, but it would have been with extremely colorful language, just to spite him...and us. Because someone deigned to tell two teenagers (or anyone else, for that matter) that they should watch their language, they would be told off at the very least, and physically harmed at worst. This is now.

I previously wrote a book called *Evil Rising,* and it was primarily about the undergirding source evil within society and where that evil is leading us. I discussed the powers, principalities, and dominions that operate in the atmospheric heavens in their attempts to turn this world completely godless. They have created such a culture, but it seems they are not done.

While my focus in my previous book was on the satanic elements that have infiltrated society, this book focuses far more on the pedestrian. We take a look at our world to see how the satanic undergirding is stripping away what has long been considered the appropriate conduct and speech, essentially replacing it with something so completely horrid that it really has become evil incarnate.

Going, going, gone is any real semblance of civility anymore. People say what they want, do what they want, and pretty much are what they want to be. If someone comes along and objects, they are either shouted down, beat down, or both. The worst aspect of this is that it has not yet reached its full potential. Things can still become far worse, and they will, if the Bible has any truth to it.

So why write a book that features gloom and doom within society when there is nothing that can be done about it? It is for the purpose of educating.

Years ago, people felt comfortable leaving their homes or cars unattended as long as the doors were locked. That sense of security is gone. Now, not only do we ensure that all of our doors, windows, and cars are locked when we are not in them, but many people have resorted to bars on those windows and doors, as well as extravagant alarm systems for their vehicles.

A few months ago, my wife parked our car in the parking lot to take the bus to work. Around midday I received a call from the local police saying our car had been broken into. When I arrived, I found that the entire back window had been smashed out, all because there were a few bags in the back that appeared they might have something worthwhile in them. There was nothing and nothing was taken.

Crimes of opportunity are becoming greater and occurring more often, and they are often becoming far more dangerous than ever before because the people doing the crimes care less about any harm that may come to the victim.

Why does this seem to be the case? I believe it has everything to do with being selfish. That may seem elementary and even too simple for some to accept, but the reality is that whenever human beings place Self on the throne, we are headed for trouble.

Today's generation of people is far more selfish than before in many ways. It is as if people have opened themselves to a form of self-centeredness that has not been heretofore known. If this is the case, where did it come from and where is it taking our society?

People are bewildered today and for good reason. They are unaware of the dangers of a self-centered society and they are clueless as to what God's Word has told us about being selfish. Most today seem completely baffled about the problems within our society and they believe that by simply creating more laws, the problems will be solved.

The problem, though, is far deeper than any man-made law can contend with, and proof of that is the fact that the laws already on the books do not keep certain people from breaking them. Laws only work for law-abiding citizens, and if everyone was law-abiding, the world would not be in the disarray it is in currently.

What's the solution? Is there an end in sight for the self-centeredness that pervades the world today? Yes, there is a solution, but most will ignore it because it is either seen as too simplistic or too confining, which merely proves that Self is alive and well in most people today.

In this book, we're going to spend some time visiting the sewer that humanity has created. We need to do that to understand the full realm of Self and how it has learned to govern just about every area of society, even many churches.

Once we see the raw sewage, we can then focus on the answer to the problem. Ultimately, though, it will be up to each individual to avail themselves of that answer. Responding to it by embracing it means a walking away from Self. Rejecting it means continuing to keep Self enthroned.

Certainly the choice is yours, but you should know up front that Self will fight you tooth and nail because it hates the idea of being replaced. Keep that in mind as we discover the truths about Self that it wants to continue to hide from you.

Fred DeRuvo, July 2011

Chapter 1
Self Changes Everything

There are a number of things happening throughout the world today. In fact, these things were set in motion quite some time ago and have merely been building to the point that exists now. The overriding factor within society is that people are *selfish*. That may come as little shock to anyone, but when we say *selfish*, most people simply think of a child throwing a tantrum when not getting his/her way.

What is prevalent throughout our global society is far worse, yet stems from the same problem. Selfishness in adults often far outweighs selfishness in children simply because, apart from the law, there is really nothing that tends to act *against* that selfishness. For lawbreakers, the law itself is no deterrent. Adults come to realize that they do not have to follow the law if they don't want to do so. Children generally do not think like that.

Selfishness at its root is when a person places themselves at the *center* of the universe, metaphorically speaking. This may start out only including one or two things in a person's life, but can and often does grow to the point of incorporating major aspects of that person's life, if not all of it.

When we are children and act according to our own natures and immaturities, we cry when things don't go our way. If we have intelligent, loving parents, those parents teach us to avoid such behavior because they know that it is not good to allow it to continue. It is not good for the child and it is not good for civilization. As we grow under such tutelage, we begin to see that life is made up of more than simply *my wants*. There is an entire society of people who have wants and needs, and if everyone is solely concerned with filling only their *own* desires and needs, the world truly becomes a completely self-centered place in which to live, with everyone vying for first place.

Again, all of this may sound like common knowledge. That's the problem, because while it *is* common knowledge to understand *how* selfishness works in a person's life as it affects society on the whole, it is far more difficult to adjust the way a person thinks about his/her own selfishness so that he/she can become an individual who gives *back* to society instead of simply taking *from* society at every turn.

I'm sure we will agree that a person who is relatively *selfless* is far more attractive – both inside and out - than the person who thinks merely about his/her own needs and how the world can meet those needs. In a child, we understand the problem and correct it if we care about that child. In some ways, a child who throws a tantrum is a bit amusing, simply because they see their problem as being more important at that time than anything or anyone else's problem. As adults we realize that the child's perspective is skewed.

When we see this behavior in adults, it is often chafing on us. In fact, many people react with anger at the obvious selfishness that is visible in other people. We become angry because we realize that they were never raised properly and likely given what they demanded as children. As they grew into adults, the same response that they were routinely met with as children became the expected norm for them. We realize that as adults, they are unable to see beyond their own *self-centeredness*. The world is here to make their life better and not the other way around.

Certainly history has gone through its cycles and periods of darkness. We are all familiar with the Dark Ages, in which things were truly dark indeed. People during that time seem to us to have been very base, living much like animals. However, in animals we excuse that behavior because we understand that they live by instinct and not through moral decision-making. Not so with human beings.

People are supposed to live their lives based on *morality*. The question then becomes, *whose* morality? Everyone has their own version of what is right and wrong, and they generally live by those standards.

However, in society today, that morality is increasingly becoming so relative that it has become dangerously close to anarchy in many areas of the world. People do what seems good to them, whether or not it is good for anyone else.

So what *is* happening in our world today? How did we get here and where are we going? Is what we see in society today merely a phase which we will move out of one day, or are we simply spiraling downward out of control, with people becoming *deliberately* more selfish than they have been in the past?

I want to look at the juxtaposition between the person who lives *for* God vs. the person who lives *for* Self. I've deliberately capitalized the word "self" in most cases because for that person, Self has literally become that individual's god. To me, Self is a living, viable entity that constantly demands our attention.

In this life, we either worship the God of the Bible or we worship Self. It's that simple. So in essence, what we will discover in this book is how those variations appear to others. On one hand, we have the person who lives for God while moving *away* from Self, and on the other hand, we have the person who lives *for* Self while moving *away* from God.

Obviously, if Scripture is true, we were not created to be selfish. Originally, Self was not enthroned. We were created to worship God and live *for* Him, which means that while we live for God, we would also be living lives that would promote peacefulness among the nations of the world. Selflessness does not engender war because true selflessness does not experience *jealousy*.

We also know that if the Bible is taken seriously and understood as truth, our first parents fell because they exercised their choice to become selfish. Satan, the master of the self-centered, came to Eve and Adam with a proposition. That proposition stated that *God* was the One who was truly being selfish, and because of His selfishness, neither Adam nor Eve could truly experience being human in all its fullness. In fact, to be fully human (according to Satan), meant to become gods ourselves.

This is the core of all temptation leading to sin. It is the desire to *feed* Self. In doing so, we become less like the God of the Bible and more like this god of this world.

Satan fell due to his own elevated opinion of himself. He stopped seeing himself as being a created individual and began to see himself as someone *self-made*. It was on this basis that sin entered into his life, and from that point onward he began to believe that he was or would become far greater than God, his Creator (cf. Isaiah 14; Ezekiel 27). He promised him*self* a number of things:

1. *"I will ascend to heaven;*
2. *I will raise my throne above the stars of God,*
3. *And I will sit on the mount of assembly; In the recesses of the north.*
4. *I will ascend above the heights of the clouds;*
5. *I will make myself like the Most High."* (Isaiah 14:13b-14)

Those five "I wills" represent the beginnings of true selfishness. Satan began to see that he could do anything, and he also began to believe that he was far greater than God. Because he saw himself as someone who was ultimately greater than God, his Creator, he wrongly believed that there was nothing beyond the limits of his ability. In spite of the fact that God has proven that notion false at every turn, Satan presses onward, desperately clinging to that false belief.

Over the centuries since his sin and fall from grace, he has spent a good deal of time tempting human beings to believe the same lie he chose to believe. He began with Adam and Eve and has continued from there.

Every sin you can think of has its root in one thing: *selfishness*. Again, that word seems almost innocuous to us – rather harmless. So what, everyone has occasional bouts with selfishness, we think. We *should* treat ourselves to the good things in life, we are told from many sources. We *should* look out for number one, because if we don't, who will?

SELF

Diagram 1

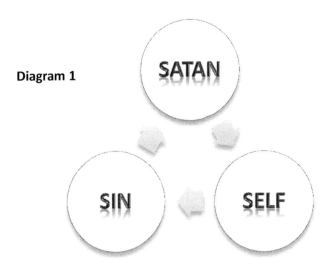

At every turn in society, the message is the same: *live your life for yourself. Get out of life what you want. If you don't do it, no one will do it for you. You were created to enjoy life. Grab all the gusto you can get!*

What can a person do when faced with an assault, which at every turn pumps up Self rather than deposes it? Most people find it too difficult to turn from that type of desire. It's too easy to give into because Self declares that type of life is exactly what is needed to find joy, happiness, and fulfillment. Give in to gain the world!

In a nutshell, there is an easy way to see this problem. Self stems

Diagram 2

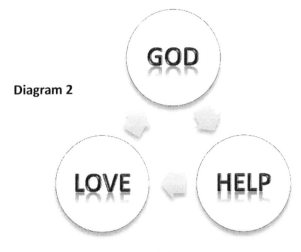

from turning *away* from God and *toward* selfish desires, desires that are meant only to serve Self. This is Satan's biggest parlor trick and he uses it often. It becomes a vicious cycle.

The simple diagrams on the previous page show us how it works. Satan causes us to sin by *presenting* us with temptations that are often seen by us as too powerful to ignore or overcome. We see the temptation as promising, even *enlightening* at times, and therefore see it as something that will *benefit* us. Yes, it *will* benefit Self, and that is what we do not see. The more we give into the power of temptation leading to sin, the greater our connection with Self will become.

The second diagram highlights the process for the individual who submits him/herself to God. In that situation, because of the individual's desire to please God, He provides the necessary help and strength to overcome the temptation, which allows the person to effectively ignore the demands of Self. This ultimately leads to living a life of love.

Just as the process for the self-centered person involves a lifetime of giving into the demands of Self, with the resultant consequences, so too does the process for the individual who strives to live for God involve a lifetime of submitting to His Lordship, with the resultant consequences.

The difference is stark, and obviously, consistency makes the huge difference. For the Christian who merely dabbles in obedience to God's will, results will be vague and undefined, as opposed to the person who consistently endeavors to submit to Christ's authority over the believer.

What is true about both diagrams is that they recognize a *process,* and each process stimulates something, either what God considers good or bad. This is exactly why those who – by their own strength –

do "good" things like being involved in charities, doing nice things for people, and other things as well, because they believe they will be blessed. If they are doing those things in their own strength, it usually stems from the demands of Self.

For instance, if a person wants to be accepted by a group of other people, that individual may begin doing things for some of the individuals in that group. They may believe that they are doing those things to simply be nice, but what is the ulterior motive? The actual motive is that they want to be *accepted* by members of that group, and currently, they are on the outside looking in.

Their "good works" then are only done because Self is saying that by doing those things, they will be accepted. When they are accepted, then Self will be satisfied – for now, until something else comes along that Self will require.

Now, consider the same situation in which someone simply does something for someone because there is a *need*, not because they know that if they do something nice, something nice will be done for them in return. So that person simply fills the need in another person's life because they are in a position to do so. They meet that need and then they go on with life. That person has not done what they did because they *wanted* something from the other person. They did what they did because a *need* existed and God had provided them with the resources to fill that need.

It's really not that easy, simply due to the fact that Self has complex ways of hiding its true motivation to us. We tend to believe some of the more altruistic ways we look at the reasons why we do things, and it is difficult sometimes to cut to the chase and believe what conscience tells us about ourselves. If you have ever been around a person who is the center of every situation, discussion, or argument, you know what I mean.

I will spend more time on this as we go through this book, but I also want to spend some amount of time on the things in life that we use to fulfill the demands of Self. We will tie this all together so that we can see the results in a clear and effective way.

Chapter 2
Self and Circumcision

That probably seems a strange title for a chapter. What's the problem with circumcision and how is that surgical act *selfish* in any way? It depends upon who you ask, but there are people who have strong reactions to circumcision.

Not long ago, actor Russell Crowe came out and blasted circumcision. On June 9th, Crowe "tweeted" the following statement: *"Circumcision is barbaric and stupid. Who are you to correct nature? Is it real that GOD requires a donation of foreskin? Babies are perfect."*[1]

---

[1] http://justjared.buzznet.com/2011/06/09/russell-crowe-circumcision-is-barbaric-and-stupid/

Actors and musicians never cease to amaze me. Sure, they're people, of course, and they are certainly allowed to have opinions, but why is it when *they* speak, much of the world goes, "*Right on!*" Frankly, it doesn't matter who says what. If it's wrong, it's wrong. More actors should offer their opinions *less* frequently because people don't generally become fans for their opinions. They become fans because of their talent. Interestingly enough, it is usually only after those actors or musicians become famous that they start offering their opinions. They didn't generally offer their opinions as they were climbing their own personal ladder of success because they didn't want to risk offending or alienating anyone. Once they became successful, they all of a sudden came to believe that they could say anything and it would be fine.

Regarding circumcision, the entire situation is so melodramatic it's not even worth discussing, and I wouldn't be discussing it except for the fact that not only Crowe, but someone in San Francisco, is trying to get circumcision outlawed by putting the question to the voting public on the next ballot. This is the same city, of course, that has outlawed the Happy Meal because of its empty calories.

Arguments abound regarding circumcision. The idea that some baby cannot agree or disagree to the unnecessary surgery is too much for some people. Does anyone see any inconsistency here? I do on a number of levels.

It seems the very same people who argue that circumcision is wrong because it's "barbaric" or "stupid" or "unnecessary" would go to bat for any woman who wanted to have an abortion. Last I heard, I know of no unborn baby that was asked if it was okay to kill it. The mother simply does what she wants because, after all, it's her body. So apparently, killing unborn babies is perfectly fine because the mother must retain the right to be able to legally murder something that is not born within her own body.

However, remove a few inches of extra skin from around the male genitalia and all hell breaks loose! This is too weird for me, and it simply shows where self-centeredness has gotten society.

San Francisco, the city by the Bay, known for its homosexuality, Alcatraz, Dirty Harry, and the Golden Gate Bridge, is fighting the good fight by eliminating both calories (in McDonald's Happy Meals) and now something it deems as "unnecessary" surgery on newborns.

But let's take a look at San Francisco for a moment. Long the bastion of overt homosexuality and events that cater to the homosexual community, while they're outlawing Happy Meals and attempting to do away with circumcision, they see no problem with sexually-charged events such as "Up Your Alley." This is an annual event where literally anything goes, and it happens right out in the open. I honestly do not feel comfortable talking about it within the confines of this book, but suffice it to say that during this event, it is common for men to walk around barely dressed or not at all dressed. They do far more than rub elbows with each other in any open doorway. Sex acts take place on street corners, in doorways, and under tent canopies right in the center of the street. It is modern-day Sodom in all its lewdness and moral bankruptcy.

It's all in good fun, though, right? The event was, at one time, blatantly sponsored by well-known beer companies, but they have toned back their *obvious* involvement because of the bad publicity they received. If you do a search on "Up Your Alley" on the 'Net (and I would *not* recommend it), you will find the official "Up Your Alley" Web site that highlights many of the (pornographic) happenings at this event. The latest one is taking place this month – July, 2011 – as I write this.

However, if you go to the official site, you will not truly see what "Up Your Alley" is all about. For that, you have to go to another Web site that has taken a great deal of heat simply because the man who runs it has uncovered the deliberately deceptive methods newspapers and TV in the Bay Area use to handle events, and he does so to show how these outlets provide an alternate opinion about something that has happened. These news bureaus do this because they have a message to get across, so slanting the news works for them.

In fact, many of the events portrayed in the news are simply incorrect as reported, and the man who owns and operates this Web site proves it and does a good job of reporting actual events, and he seems to have little to no partisanship in doing so. He is merely interested in getting the truth out. His Web site is Zombietime.com; however, I would *strongly* caution the reader against going to that site, and please know ahead of time that going to this man's Web site will reveal events like "Up Your Alley" in all their disgusting, degrading clarity. You will see things that will likely cause you to want to wash your eyes with disinfectant, so please be warned. He has taken great pains to ensure that someone cannot simply (or accidentally) see things that they do not wish to see. Pictures are blurred out, etc., and that tends to keep things far more "PG" to "R" rated, as opposed to "X" rated. At the same time, there are some other very worthwhile (and "G" rated) areas of this man's Web site about events that have taken place that show the hypocrisy of the establishment in the Bay Area, like "Earth Day" at the Berkeley Campus. These pictures are interesting, to say the least.

So why do events such as "Up Your Alley" take place, while at the same time, there is a movement to eradicate circumcision and try to dress up San Francisco a bit by making it appear as if they care about a child's health where Happy Meals are concerned? Well, for one thing, it is considered "hateful" to discuss homosexuality in a negative light. Homosexuals don't like that, and even those homosexuals who enjoy the proclivities on display at "Up Your Alley" would refrain from speaking against it if it is not the sort of thing they involve themselves with for fear of reprisals.

But it is fine for Russell Crowe to complain about circumcision. In fairness to Crowe, he did apologize for his comments regarding circumcision, so I guess we should let him off the hook. The problem, though, is that there is something larger at work here, in my opinion.

What *one* group is generally known for circumcision? Jewish people, of course. In essence, then, the attack on circumcision is an attack on Judaism. Can you imagine if Muslims practiced circumcision? I don't believe there would be this type of talk against the act. I certainly could be wrong, but generally speaking, because people do not want to anger Muslims, they tend to back away from discussing things that serve to anger them. The list of things that can and often do anger radical Muslims seems to grow longer every day.

I recall when our son was born. Our desire was to have him circumcised, and our doctor at that point did everything he could to try to talk us out of it. We insisted, but the idea that anyone would try to dissuade us from doing what we felt was important to do is ridiculous. Even those within the medical field have taken a different look at circumcision as something that can protect people against certain sexually-transmitted diseases, or at least make it more difficult to get. Of course, if people were not promiscuous, sexually-transmitted diseases would not exist. That also has its roots in Self.

The world today is becoming far more self-centered than ever, and I believe that is clearly predicted in the Bible. If we simply consider Paul's words to Timothy, we have a very good picture of what the world was to look like during the end times. *"For men will be lovers of self, lovers of money, boastful, arrogant, revilers, disobedient to parents, ungrateful, unholy"* (2 Timothy 2:3).

Don't those words of Paul's describe civilization today? The word *civilization* is not something that should be used any longer to describe society, because we seem far from civilized. However, if we consider the fact that Paul said that men will be lovers of SELF *first*, and that everything else would generate from that, we begin to understand why people have become the way they have become. For a person to want more money, to boast about themselves, to become filled with arrogance and pride, to hate what is good, to go through life with an attitude of entitlement and to be ungrateful and the furthest thing from holy all stems from being self-centered. It means that Self is fully enthroned and all Self does is demand more than it has, never being satisfied because there is always something more Self wants to possess.

All problems of society can be boiled down to the fact that people are selfish and growing more selfish with each passing day. The more Self reigns supreme, the greater the problems that will exist in society. No amount of new laws will make society better. They will simply point out how many *more* laws selfish people can break.

Society arrived at a turning point some time ago, and eagerly passed that point, fully embracing the idea and belief that we are gods and can do anything we want to do. Because of this, our culture – globally – has become far darker and will become darker still until we reach the darkest point in all of human history – the *Tribulation* period. We're certainly coming to that point, and it seems that we cannot get there quickly enough.

What other areas of society do people indulge in by capitalizing on the fact that Self seeks its own desires? We'll discuss that in the next chapter.

Chapter 3

Self and Abortion

Now here's a subject that can and often does bring out the worst in people. Very few people are on the fence regarding this issue. Most people – 57% – believe that abortion should be legal in all states of the United States in most or all cases.[2]

The issue of abortion is a very polarizing one, yet at the same time, few people have a problem with calling murder a crime. Over the years since Roe v. Wade, though, murder has been redefined where the unborn are concerned. Instead of even focusing on the unborn child, the focus has turned to the mother and her alleged right to do

---

[2] http://abcnews.go.com/sections/us/DailyNews/abortion_poll030122.html (6/11/11)

whatever she wants to do with *her body*. This has also been shored up and strengthened because of the view that the unborn baby is nothing more than *fetal tissue*. So the unborn child is simply a fetal blob that cannot survive outside of the womb by itself, therefore no one is actually destroying *life*. Because of that belief, it has become perfectly acceptable for a woman to rid herself of this unwanted fetal tissue.

Again, the sole focus of the abortion debate is the *mother*. The child does not enter into the debate at all – unless the mother *wants* the unborn child. At that point, *fetal tissue* becomes a *viable child*. It is only at the point that the mother actually *wants* to keep the unborn baby does that baby become *human*, at least as far as those who support abortion are concerned.

Yet, the fascinating part of this can be seen in the court system and the number of cases that have come through those courts over the years where a criminal perpetrated a crime against a woman who was pregnant at the time. In certain crimes, both mother and unborn child were killed. The prosecution then charged the perpetrator with *two* murders, much to the chagrin of certain women's groups who felt that this would set a precedent for the view that an unborn mass of fetal tissue might possibly be seen as human.

People get around this by claiming that the unborn fetal tissue is *potentially human*, and apparently only becomes human after it is born, or is something that the carrying mother *wants* to keep, as noted.

Do you see what has taken place over the decades? In order to assuage the guilt that often goes with killing another human being (especially one who cannot speak for him/herself), instead of seeing it for what it is, Self finds a way to let people off the hook. Self does this by refocusing attention from, in this case, the unborn baby to the mother. The emphasis then becomes what the mother truly wants to do with her *body*, not what she *will* be doing to another human being *within* her body. Proponents of rights for women who believe that a woman should have the right to kill any and every unborn child she does not want knew that they could not win the "it's murder" argument, so they removed it from the discussion and simply chose to focus on the woman and her right to choose.

I would agree that a woman has a right to choose, but in my view, she has a right to choose whether or not to either a) have sex with a man, or b) to become impregnated or not. Once pregnant, she does not have the right to choose to kill the unborn child she is carrying. That is murder. I realize that a pregnancy caused by rape is a very difficult issue to deal with, as is the issue of very young girls who become impregnated without wanting to do so. These are difficult areas to be sure, but I am referring to the fact that most women who have abortions use it as a means of birth control.

For those who argue that an unborn child (or fetal tissue as they prefer to call him/her) cannot sustain itself and will not live outside the womb for any length of time, the same can be said for a child that comes to full term and is born a healthy baby girl or boy. Go ahead and take that newborn, healthy child and simply ignore it. Don't feed it, don't change its diapers, and don't give it any liquid at all. What will happen? Of course it will die a very unpleasant death. No one in their right mind would treat a child like that, and no one in their right mind would argue that deliberately doing something like that would not constitute murder.

Yet because there is an unborn child growing within the mother's womb, it is fine to kill it because of the faulty argument that says he/she would not be able to live long outside the womb anyway. Who thinks like this except someone who is exceedingly self-centered?

Self focuses on *convenience*. The road to convenience is often the road most traveled, and Self leads the way. Why is it – if women truly have the right to choose what happens to their bodies – that abortions are often *repeat* abortions? By that I mean that more often than not, women use abortion repeatedly as a method of birth control. The same women are having the abortions, with a growing number of new girls and women entering that area every year. It is somehow easier for a girl or woman to have an abortion, rather than do what is necessary to keep from *becoming* pregnant in the first place. Why? Convenience.

I know of no woman who can become pregnant without the seed from the male. Just because a woman can now go to a fertilization specialist and become artificially inseminated does *not* remove the male from the equation. All it does is make the male an "anonymous donor." The woman was still unable to impregnate herself, all by herself, with chemicals from within her own body.

If that was the case, then maybe, *maybe*, there might be some merit in arguing that a woman has the right to choose. This is not the case, however, because a woman cannot become pregnant without the help of the male seed. It is impossible.

In a recent case, a New Mexico man took out a huge billboard advertisement protesting the fact that his ex-girlfriend opted for an abortion without telling him or even asking him about it. The situation resulted only in the woman taking the man to court for invasion of privacy and harassment.[3] So the woman was able to allegedly end the life of a human being that she had only a hand in creating and was able to do so in spite of the fact that the father had no say about it. But notice what Self *then* prompted the woman to do. Self insisted that she blame the ex-boyfriend for her pain and

---

[3] http://www.brownsvilleherald.com/articles/billboard-127517-boyfriend-jilted.html (6/11/11)

suffering. As I write this, it is still going through the courts, with the latest decision being that the man was ordered to remove the billboard. He is refusing to do so, on pain of incarceration. The argument is that the billboard invades the woman's privacy, but her name is not mentioned on the billboard at all. People who know the man would know of the woman.

This is the way Self works. It does whatever it feels is necessary to gain access to the things it wants. When Self does something that backfires on the individual where Self is enthroned, Self continues the debacle by making a bad situation worse, as in this case.

The man referred to above will never see the child he helped create because of the alleged selfishness of his ex-girlfriend. I'm not saying, by the way, that intercourse outside of marriage is fine. That is a separate issue, also brought about by Self. The problem was fully exacerbated because Self only wants what it wants. Whatever serves Self's purposes are the very things it wants.

Abortion began as an issue of murder. It has become an issue of control and choice. Arguments are put forth (with the necessary allotment of alligator tears) that a woman should have a right to choose and taking away that right puts the woman in jeopardy because she will be forced to look for illegal means of getting rid of the fetal tissue she carries.

If people were not so self-centered, abortion would not even be an issue. It *is* an issue because Self wants what it wants. Self says, "*Yes, have as much sex as you want! Don't worry about taking precautions so that you don't become pregnant! Just **go for it** and then deal with life as it happens!*"

That is how Self dictates its desires. Ultimately, Self destroys, because we were not created by God to *be* self-centered. Quite the opposite is true, but Satan has gained our ear and will do everything in his power to cause us to believe that fulfilling all the desires of Self is the pathway to freedom!

Chapter 4

Self and Gay Rights

Approximately forty years ago, the Gay Rights movement began in New York. Interestingly enough, it seems to have come full circle with New York State being the latest (the sixth) to succumb to the pressure of the Gay and Lesbian taskforces with the passage of a same-sex marriage law. It has certainly become politically *incorrect* to stand opposed to same-sex marriage and Gay rights in general.

We will likely watch more states give way to the pressure to recognize same-sex marriages as being on par with the Civil Rights movement of the 50s and 60s.

To me, this is a tragedy. It is not because I hate gay people. I don't hate them. It is not because I see them as being that much more of a sinner than I am. I'm sure gay people have always been around. The problem comes when what is done privately moves out into the open.

Previously, I referenced an annual event called "Up Your Alley" that occurs in San Francisco. There is information on the 'Net about the event, what it entails and the reason it exists. The truth of the matter is that for the average person, what goes on at this event is simply revolting. Gay people would say it's too bad that people react to that event like that. They should just stay away.

Trouble is, let's turn it around for a moment and instead of gay men being the focal point of "Up Your Alley," we had a Hedonism-type of event where heterosexuals could gather and do the same things that these gay men in San Francisco do. What would happen?

Well, for one thing, the heterosexual people would be arrested for lewd and lascivious conduct involving sex in public, which includes, of course, the things that heterosexuals do behind closed doors. Somehow, though, when gay men are involved, it's a different story. In spite of the fact that X-rated activities occur out in the open, the police, the officials, and even the mayor of San Francisco turn a blind eye to those activities. No one is arrested, unless of course there is criminal violence.

It doesn't matter that what is being done during "Up Your Alley" is illegal to do out in the open. It doesn't matter that large groups of grown men walk around in the streets nearly or all nude, parading up and down the street, passing vendors and police officers alike.

This type of activity, when allowed publicly, is repugnant. I believe it is this type of thing that opens the door to God's judgment. I also believe as we see more states swing wide the door to legalize same-sex marriage we can expect to see more problems rise in the world.

I also believe, though legislators downplay the possibility, that we can eventually expect lawsuits to take place against churches and ministers if those churches and ministers are unwilling to perform same-sex ceremonies.

In New York State, one of the sticking points to passage of the law was that some legislators were concerned for this very thing. They must have worked things out because the bill to allow same-sex marriage passed. This, however, does *not* mean that people will not eventually try to sue churches and ministers who refuse to perform same-sex marriage ceremonies. In fact, I strongly believe it will happen.

In some ways, the Gay and Lesbian taskforces that have been working diligently are similar to thugs. Not all of them, certainly, but there are groups like Queer Nation who get in people's faces. They are not above making their points by disrupting services, legislator meetings and whatnot, solely to get their point across. Some of what they do certainly borders on violence. They are militant in their stand against the conservative position that does not want to see same-sex marriage legalized.

As more states open the door to same-sex unions, the pressure will be on for churches to recognize and/or perform these ceremonies. If they don't, they will likely experience protests *in* their churches by groups like Queer Nation. These folks don't mind being arrested because it furthers their position by bringing more attention to it.

I fully believe that there will come a time when churches will be sued for their unwillingness to perform same-sex marriage ceremonies. I also wonder what door will open next. Right now, the focus is on same-sex unions. When that gains enough momentum, will we begin to see a push to legalize man-on-boy relationships? What about transgender issues? How will they make their way into the legal arena?

We are seeing an absolute change in society today. With New York's passage of same-sex unions, it has become the sixth and largest state to make these unions legal.

Governor Cuomo said, "*We made a powerful statement...This state is at its finest when it is a beacon of social justice.*"[4] So now Cuomo and those who voted *for* same-sex unions become the heroes. You can bet that gays and lesbians throughout the state will work to re-elect these individuals to office.

Interestingly enough, it was a lone Democrat who stood against same-sex unions. Democratic Sen. Ruben Diaz (a Bronx minister) stated, "*God, not Albany, settled the issue of marriage a long time ago...I'm sorry you are trying to take away my right to speak...Why are you ashamed of what I have to say?*"[5] God bless that man.

I believe it was Chuck Missler who stated in one of his books that it wasn't the sin of sodomy for which God destroyed Sodom and Gomorrah. It was because the sin was so blatantly out in the open (my paraphrase of Dr. Missler's words). I would have to agree because it would appear that with the door being forced open like this, how is it possible to stop *anything* from becoming legal and therefore normalized?

Gay people fully believe that they were *born* gay. The problem with that is that many have come out of that lifestyle and now live a perfectly heterosexual lifestyle. Joe Dallas and many others have written books detailing their lives while involved in the gay lifestyle

---

[4] http://www.msnbc.msn.com/id/43507672/ns/politics-more_politics/?gt1=43001
[5] Ibid

as well as after leaving it. Are these just mixed-up people? Are they exceptions to the rule?

The truth is that if God created Adam and Eve, He did so in order for them to procreate after their kind. Two men together cannot procreate and neither can two women. Men and women need each other, but, of course, for more than simply procreation. As much as gays and lesbians argue that they are born as homosexuals, nature seems to defy that statement.

I believe that once things become mainstreamed that should not be mainstreamed, society has turned a corner from which it cannot return. The world leaders want homosexual unions legalized for a number of reasons. Normally, homosexuals adopt, rather than have their own children. This means that homosexuals do not add to the population, but simply take from the existing population and add the children to their own family.

Another reason I believe world leaders want same-sex unions legitimized is because it helps to create chaos. It moves the world toward a new world order, one that these world leaders hope will replace the existing one.

Much of America is still deeply entrenched in biblical principles and beliefs. These world leaders know that it will take a lot to move people from their staunch biblical beliefs to a humanistic stance. The way to do that is through social upheaval that ultimately overwhelms society.

If world leaders can create such a wave of change that it will impact everything that conservatives hold near and dear, they believe they will go a long way in creating the change necessary to usher in the new world order. What people do not realize is that this new world order is nothing more than recreating the world so that only a few –

all on the same team, of course – control *everything*. Right now, that is not the case.

Once world leaders are able to make this happen, they – as a group – will have absolute power over all things. This is why they have been doing what they have been doing. It is the greatest form of Self worship that has ever existed. Throughout the ages, these leaders – changing with each generation, but remaining within the same power families – have done what they could to inch the world along to the global change that is necessary so that current society can literally be overthrown, replaced with *their* view of what works – for *them*.

When I was growing up, my dad would point out commercials in which the wife/mother always knew more than the father/husband. Usually, the man was white, because if you make fun of white men, who is going to complain?

That still continues to this day, and in my opinion, it is even *more* blatant. I saw a commercial for a computer repair company the other day, in which the (white) husband was using his computer and something went wrong. He complained, got up, and started out the door. His beautiful wife stopped him and asked him what was wrong. He explained he was having computer problems. Never fear, because WIFE is here! She immediately went over to his laptop and with a few strokes of the keys – voila! – the computer was fixed. The husband was dumbfounded and, of course, marveled at how much money his wife had just saved him. No problem, because she was heading out to the door to go *shopping*!

Whenever I see a company that runs an ad like that, I make a determination not to use them. They are insulting me and all men, so why should I give them my money?

Self is growing more emboldened at every turn. By following its dictates, world leaders are doing their best to bring this world to the edge of chaos in order to create a new world order that allows their "self" to reign supreme.

The interesting thing here is that Daniel explains how this will look. Once the world's economy collapses, a group of ten "kingdoms" will rise up to take control of the entire world by breaking it up into ten sections. Can you see a problem already? You can read about these in Daniel 2, 7, and Revelation 13 and 17. I cannot imagine that ten leaders will work together smoothly.

In fact, they don't, because from the ten, an eleventh one rises. *"As for the ten horns, out of this kingdom ten kings will arise; and another will arise after them, and he will be different from the previous ones and will subdue three kings"* (Daniel 7:24). Those ten "horns" simply represent leaders or kings of those ten kingdoms. Notice that another one rises from among them. This one is the Antichrist. He is the eleventh, but because he "subdues" three of them, he is also the "eighth" of Revelation 17:11.

You see, right now, the world leaders are all working together to create that world order they have been yearning for, and because of that, they work in harmony. Those who are not part of the elite are the enemy, so the world leaders have a common enemy.

However, when they succeed in bringing in the new world order over which they will rule, they will no longer have an enemy outside of themselves. The enemy will become one another. Unfortunately for them, because they have been focusing on an enemy *outside* of their circle, they will not notice that the "eleventh" is among them.

This "eleventh" will sit back while they do all the work to bring about a new world order that rises from the chaos they create. Once that happens, this "eleventh" (the Antichrist) will step up, subdue three (probably by killing them) and will claim ultimate authority. The remaining seven of the original ten "kings" will announce their loyalty to the "eleventh," which is now the "eighth." They're not stupid, having no death wish.

So you see how deceptive Self can be. Because of the work that these world leaders are doing, they are creating havoc and chaos in global society. Whether it's promoting abortion or the continued funding of Planned Parenthood; legalizing same-sex marriages; outspending what our government takes in; sending jobs overseas; prohibiting offshore oil drilling, yet encouraging other nations to do that with U.S. tax dollars; or even doing absolutely nothing when there is black-on-white crime as we are seeing in growing trends throughout the U.S.; it's all done for the same purpose – to create *chaos*.

Are you starting to see the picture? Self is thoroughly destructive and it never leaves a person unscathed. Self is the most destructive idol that exists, and those who are in direct control of world affairs are serving Self exclusively.

All the social problems we are seeing and experiencing in this world are due to the fact that the world leaders are busy creating these problems to get our minds off of the fact that one day, they will be in charge. When that happens, the world will realize just how badly they have been fooled. It will absolutely be too late, though.

If I were a humanist, I would probably be concerned. If I was not an authentic believer, I would have reason to be afraid. If I was simply a political conservative with no moorings in the biblical revelation and God Himself, I would likely be in abject fear.

However, as I see things in the works, I comfort myself knowing that God is fully in control. He allows/designs these things to occur to bring *His* goals to fruition. In order for the Lord to return in His second coming at the end of the Tribulation, the Tribulation *must* take place. In order for Him to vanquish evil and imprison Satan for 1,000 years, He must physically return to this earth and set up His

Kingdom. It cannot happen unless the full evil of the Tribulation plays itself out. Far from simply being a time of tremendously unbridled evil, multitudes will come to know the Lord in salvation. God will use all that Satan can throw at the world for His good and ultimately for His glory. Though the horrors of the Tribulation will be great and the darkness ever-present, the light of God's salvation will never be extinguished once during that period of time. God will save all who will come to Him in submission and repentance.

There are some terrible things ahead of us, all because of Self. However, Self does not gain the final and ultimate victory. In the end, Self is denied by the God of the universe. *That* is worth celebrating!

Chapter 5

Self and Money

How many times have you heard the statement, "*Money is the root of all evil*"? You've probably heard it as many times as I have, but it is *not* an accurate statement. Like many things in Scripture, that saying has been taken completely out of context and misquoted.

The statement is actually, "*For the love of money is the root of all evil,*" and that is found in 1 Timothy 6:10. Here is the entire verse: "*For the love of money is a root of all sorts of evil, and some by longing for it have wandered away from the faith and pierced themselves with many griefs.*"

Loving something inordinately is far different from simply knowing or appreciating its value, or having and using something to fulfill a legitimate *need*. We all need money to buy things so that we and our families can survive. We all need jobs so that we have money to buy those things we need. Most of us are content to work for our wages and are happy to have enough to make ends meet *without* having to be millionaires.

However, besides those content with what they have, there are many within society that fall into one of three categories with respect to money:

1. *Can never have enough money*
2. *Would rather steal it than work for it*
3. *Go through life with a sense of entitlement*

There are those who are very rich people in this world, and yet they seem as if they are not satisfied with the amount of money they possess. They always want more. They are workhorses as far as finding ways of making more money is concerned. These people can never relax, nor can they stop in their attempts to amass as much money as possible. It *drives* them in their decision-making processes.

Then you have the individuals who would rather take their chances of getting caught trying to steal money than be caught dead *working* for a living. These people have no patience with the time clock, and for them the weekly or bi-weekly paycheck just doesn't cut it. They want their money now, and they want lots of it. They also do not want to pay taxes on any money they obtain.

The third category of individual is the one who is very lazy. They have neither the energy nor the wherewithal to go out and earn a living, and they stay away from a life of crime because they don't want to go to jail. So, these folks play the system. They take on the attitude (often handed down from one generation to another) that they are entitled to take from the government so that they can live.

If these people do not get what they have come to believe they deserve, someone is going to pay! Who does the government think it is, anyway? Doesn't the government know that they *must* supply the needs of that person or that person's family?

My mother often reminded me that years ago, men in this country were too proud to take a handout from the government, so the government (during the days after the Great Depression had set in) set up jobs so that the men would be doing something, even if that something was picking up trash in parks or painting public benches. The men in those days wanted to earn a living, not simply be given a handout from the government.

Not too many years ago, a number of states considered the idea of doling out welfare checks in exchange for *work*. People who got welfare would have to do some type of work for the county or city that essentially gave back in order to quality to receive their welfare checks. Well, the amount of protesting that occurred shouldn't have surprised me, but it did. Some of the people even carried signs that said "*We shouldn't have to work for our welfare!*" or something similar.

So why is this? By now, you know the answer is because of Self. Why do people love money inordinately? Again, it is due to the demands of Self. Why do people commit crimes? For no other reason than because of Self.

Money itself is *not* the root of all evil. Loving money is the root of all evil because it causes people to do things that they might not do if they did not love money. People who love money do many things for it that they would not otherwise do, including breaking the law, or adopting the attitude of entitlement.

Rich people who feel the need to get richer are also simply being obedient to Self. The problem with Self, of course, is that Self never has enough. It can never be satisfied because there is always something more out there that Self will get a person to believe he/she must have. By obtaining it, they are feeding Self within them. In time, Self will need something else and then the person is forced to go out and find a way to obtain it in order to keep Self happy. In the process, they become miserable, because all they really are is a slave to Self. Self reigns supreme and the person who succumbs to Self is nothing more than a slave to it.

In the verse we quoted from 1 Timothy 6, please notice that Paul tells Timothy that *loving* money above all things will eventually drag people away from the faith, and they will wind up harming themselves a great deal.

I don't believe that Paul is speaking of a loss of salvation here at all. Living by faith is an act of our will. We live by faith or we live by Self, and Christians are not exempt. The difference between the authentic Christian and the non-Christian is that the Christian has within him/her the capacity to *ignore* Self because of the indwelling Holy Spirit. He will provide me with the power to ignore Self *if* I ask Him to help me.

The Christian can just as easily pay attention to the demands of Self and wind up following Self down that road. By doing so, that person is not living by faith, but by Self. God will only allow that for so long, though.

So what Paul is saying here is that the person who is a Christian can easily become entangled in the affairs and cares of this world solely because he/she chooses to listen to Self, eventually chasing the dictates of Self, rather than submitting to the Lord.

Christians are not exempt from sinning, nor are they always going to perfectly ignore the demands of Self all the time. Ideally, every Christian should consistently avoid following the lead of Self because of the empowerment of the indwelling Holy Spirit. This is not something that any Christian will ever do perfectly in this life. When we fail, we must acknowledge our sin to God, get up (or turn around) and once again begin following the Lord by submitting our will to Him. Self will not give in quietly, but Self is a fully defeated foe that we do not have to acknowledge, much less follow.

Nowhere more than in the areas of money are the demands of Self made more clear. There are a tremendous number of toys that can be purchased with money. The more money a person has, the more toys they can buy.

My wife and I have two cars and I have a motorcycle. They are all paid off completely. Neither one of us ever want another car payment. We would prefer to spend money fixing our vehicles rather than have a monthly car payment that routinely lasts up to five to seven years these days. On a $20,000 car, a person will be paying an additional $5,000 in interest by the time they pay off that car over the five years of the loan. That's five thousand dollars that you are paying for the privilege of taking a loan from the bank or credit union.

We just had a number of things repaired on one of our cars, which cost us a total of about $1,600. One of the things that we had done was to have our differential replaced. Fortunately for us, we have a very good and honest mechanic who works out of his home. If we had taken our vehicle to the dealer or some other station, our brake job that our mechanic did for roughly $500 would have cost us about $1,200, which is quite a savings to us. What we paid out, we paid out once. This is not a recurring payment like a loan would be.

It is to our best interest to keep our cars in working order for as long as possible. Sure, we could go out and purchase some new vehicle that costs $20,000 to $30,000 or more, but why? We have no desire to be strapped like that and neither of us cares how expensive or good looking the car may happen to be.

We work hard for the money we earn and we want it to go as far as possible. Buying a new car just because having a new car would be "cool" or "exciting" is not reason enough for us to buy one. This is the same type of reasoning that got this nation where it is now. Our nation is in dire straits today because of the love of money and the overspending that people have participated in, all because of the demands of Self.

So the question to ask yourself is this: does money rule over you? Do you constantly have to have latest item, whether it's a cell phone, video game, video game console, car, or something else? Do you also find that once you have these new things, the thrill tends to wear off rather quickly? If so, that's because Self has demanded that you buy it because *Self* wants it. As soon as you get it, Self is fine for a short while, then like a pack rat, Self sees the next thing on the horizon and begins working on you to obtain it, somehow, some way.

For years, whenever I had an idea about something, I tended to put it into practice. After all, they all seemed like good ideas to me, so why wait?

What I have learned now is that when I get an idea, I *wait*. I do some research and then if the idea is still there a week, or two, or even a month later, then chances are that it was a good idea. Most of the time, I have found that these ideas I have, while good ideas, are things that I realize I can put off obtaining or doing for some time.

Self loves to keep us busy chasing one thing or another, but have you ever noticed how tiring that can be, as well as unsatisfying? Self could care less about that, though, because Self sees you as there to serve Self, not the other way around.

Loving money can *really* set you back.

Chapter 6

Self and Boasting

No one likes to be ignored. If other people don't notice things in us that we believe are worthwhile, we'll tell them somehow, some way. This tendency to boast is something that comes from thinking more highly of Self than we should. It is a fact that people do not like hanging around someone who spends their time boasting about their abilities. They often find people like that *obnoxious* due to their perceived arrogance. People's reactions to boasters can range from rolling the eyes, to walking away, or laughing at them behind their back.

The funniest thing is often that these boasters seem not to notice those reactions. The reason is simply because they are so engrossed with themselves that they really are unable to see what's going on around them. They have become blind, and Self is the very thing that has blinded them.

One of my favorite movies is a Sci-Fi spoof in the vein of *Star Trek* called *Galaxy Quest*. It has a great cast and the script itself is funny. Sometimes, I wonder how actors come up with their character, as in the case of Enrico Colantoni who played the character Mathesar. Mathesar and his compadres are aliens called "Thermians." They appear as human (using their own technology) and speak English (in a haltingly weird, sing-song way) so that their human counterparts will accept and understand them.

Tim Allen plays character Jason Nesmith, a decidedly Captain Kirk type of role. In the movie, Nesmith is seen with his fellow actors long after the show *Galaxy Quest* has been cancelled from the airwaves, attending the obligatory Sci-Fi conventions, yucking it up with fans and providing autographs. He obviously loves the attention and adulation he continually receives in spite of the fact that the show that made him famous is long over and he has done nothing new since then. He lives off of his past success. Besides conventions, he also does guest appearances at store openings.

During one convention, he excuses himself to go to the men's room. While he is in one of the stalls, two attendees from the show also stop in, and while there, are heard making derogatory remarks specifically about Nesmith and how he is unable to see that people are actually making fun of him. This is shocking to Nesmith, who remains in the stall for a few minutes after they leave, to the sounds of their fading laughter.

That was a wake-up call for Nesmith. He had never considered the fact that people didn't think he was as fantastic as he thought himself.

He had not given any thought to the possibility that at least some fans were actually making fun of him while merely pretending to take him seriously. Such was the blow to his ego.

This is often the way the boastful person reacts to the news that he or she is not as appealing to others as they are to themselves. It is with disbelief at first, then not long after that, the disbelief can change to anger and resentment.

The problem, though, is that in the case of an egotistical person who feels the need to boast, Self has taught them that they are *more* important than others and should see themselves in such a way. Because of this, Self has succeeded in becoming the center of that person's universe. The person, though, does not realize that once again, they have merely become enslaved to Self, providing the energy and doing the very things that Self wants done in order to remain in its elevated position.

Boasting is something that draws attention to Self. The more a person boasts, the more they *will* boast. That is a cycle that continues without let–up, unless the person personally intervenes to break that cycle.

Since boasting draws attention to Self, it is clear from many areas of Scripture that the very act of boasting is anathema to God. The only permissible boasting is when we boast in Jesus and what He has accomplished for us. This is what Paul did. In Galatians 6:14, Paul stated, *"But may it never be that I would boast, except in the cross of our Lord Jesus Christ, through which the world has been crucified to me, and I to the world."* If we understand the context of Paul's words, he was arguing against the need to be circumcised. Judaizers had wormed their way into the church at Galatia and they were teaching that being a "Christian" was fine, *but* it was very important that the laws of Judaism be upheld in order to find favor with God. This meant that the men in that church should be circumcised to fulfill the covenant requirements of God as given to Moses.

Paul was essentially telling the Galatian believers (among other things) that while being circumcised had merit as far as the world was concerned (it allowed *boasting* in the flesh), it not only offered nothing as far as God was concerned, but ultimately put the Galatian believers back under the law. This meant that they would be relying on the acts of the flesh for salvation, as opposed to the authentic salvation that comes only through faith (and nothing else) in Jesus and His atoning work.

This is why Paul says he boasted in Jesus, because he was in effect boasting in what God had accomplished for him. Circumcision can cause the individual to boast in themselves and in their own acts that they believe *add* to or aid them in obtaining salvation.

In the book *History of the Church, Vol. 6, pp. 408-409*, Joseph Smith, founder of Mormonism, boasted that he actually did far more than Jesus did with respect to the Church. *"I am the only man that has ever been able to keep a whole church together since the days of Adam."* Smith says a great deal more than that, but that one sentence sums up his belief in himself, in Paul, in all the prophets, and in Jesus. Clearly, Smith saw himself as greater than all of them put together.

Boasting takes our eyes and places them squarely on Self. It very quickly becomes obnoxious to hear people brag about themselves or even someone else. This self-aggrandizing behavior exhibited by many within the world today reeks of pride and false humility.

How many times have we listened to the speeches given by celebrities or politicians, only to hear how wonderful this person or that person is? How often have preachers extolled the virtues of some dearly departed relative or friend of the family as if they were nearly the living embodiment of perfection itself?

The truth of the matter is that we rarely see things from God's perspective because we are too busy focusing on Self, which sits squarely on the throne of our life. We fail to understand that we are not what we think we are, and neither is anyone else. How can we be, if God says that our heart is so wicked, it is impossible to know (cf. Jeremiah 17:9), and that all of our good works and righteousness are as filthy rags (cf. Isaiah 64:4-9)?

Boasting in ourselves or someone else keeps us from seeing life from God's perspective. It can actually keep us from evangelizing the lost because we may fool ourselves into thinking that they are "good" people and God loves them.

No, they are not truly good as God defines good, and yes, God loves them. He loves them to the point that He was willing to become human to die for them. However, something is required of them. They must be willing to stop boasting in their own flesh, their own ideas, and their talents, none of which they created. Once they stop boasting in themselves, they may then begin to see that they are not as great as they believe they are, and can then start to see the truth that they are actually in need of a Savior.

Because I spent some time acting in plays, my heart tends to go out to people in the acting world who *seem* like nice people. However, that is their public persona. We do not know what they are actually like unless they have a public meltdown (or unless we get to know them personally), which becomes fodder for the magazines and newspapers that cater to that sort of thing.

Ultimately, no matter how talented someone is, they *still* need God and the only salvation that is available. It is unfortunate when I see an actor or actress who appears to be a natural in front of the camera because it is often impossible for them to see that God sends rain and sunlight on the just and the unjust (cf. Matthew 5:34). God gives talent to people who are His and who are not His. He does this because He loves humanity. The need still exists that each and every person should make a decision *for* Jesus.

Too many people pat themselves on the back when they have used their talent(s) successfully. Did they create that talent? No, but they too often believe they did.

I have played drums for years. I enjoy music. I am creative. Yet, I did not design myself with these things. God gave me musical abilities. He built within me the deep interest I have to write and create artistically. All I have done is fan it into a flame, but I cannot take credit for the talents I possess, no more than I can take credit for how tall I am, or what color I hair I was born with, or which gender I am. Those things were and remain in God's hands.

Had I never pushed myself to learn to play drums, I would still have a strong desire to be involved in music in some way. The same applies to my ability to write and create or design. I cannot take credit for these aptitudes. To do so would be a lie because I had no hand in them. I can practice to become a *better* drummer, writer, or designer, but no amount of practice is going to make me really good at these things if the basic talent and interest was not there from the beginning.

Boasting in ourselves is a sign of being *self-made*. This is inaccurate because we are *not* self-made. We are *not* gods. We are human beings, created in God's image. As such, we have a Creator, and that Creator deserves all the glory and credit for having made us.

People who learn the habit of boasting in Self become increasingly more preoccupied with Self. The reason is because once we begin to focus on Self, Self wants more of our time, our energy, and our attention. Self is never satisfied and will always want more than it has.

People who become self-centered see the world from their perspective. Rather than loving your neighbor as yourself, people who are occupied with pleasing Self wind up loving themselves as they want their neighbors to love *them*. This is tragic not only because it alienates God from us, but reverses the way that God intended us to be.

This is what society has come to mean. It is made up of people – by and large – who think very highly of their inner Self, and because of that have come to believe that they are above the law, that they can do no wrong, and life was put here for them, not the other way around.

Self has a million and one ways to boast. To Self, it all sounds so reasonable and honest. Yet it is the furthest thing from the truth.

Satan began life as the highest being God ever created. As Lucifer, he was the being immediately under God; yet at the same time, he was nowhere near the level of God's supremacy. God rules over *all* things, without exception.

In Luke 11:20, we read, "*But if I cast out demons by the finger of God, then the kingdom of God has come upon you.*" This is really a fascinating statement by Jesus. Jesus is retorting to the religious leaders who claimed He cast out demons by the power of Satan. This is ludicrous, of course, but not only did Jesus *say* that it was, but notice He says that He casts out demons with the *finger* of God, meaning very little effort is used.

Recently, the pastor of the church we attend gave the first in a series of sermons on God's attributes. He noted that nowhere in Scripture could he find a place where God exerted more energy than moving His arm (or sometimes, both arms). Most of the things God does require little to no effort on His part. Here, it becomes clear that God controls Satan and his minions with the flick of His finger. That is how insignificant Satan's power is compared to God's power.

Yet, it was this being who formulated a plan to raise his throne above God. Lucifer began boasting about his own powers, as if he had actually created himself, or better yet, was always there as God has always been there.

Boasting creates blindness. The person who spends time bragging about their attributes, the talents they believe they possess, and all other things related to Self literally blinds themselves to the truth that they need salvation. They are not as good as they think they are and the need for salvation proves it.

One of the problems, though, is that people routinely compare themselves with *other* people. We also normally compare ourselves with people who are often *less* talented than we are in an area. This makes us feel that much more important.

We will compare ourselves with a criminal and feel good that we have never been arrested, or done anything that required us to be arrested. That makes us *better*, we believe.

We compare ourselves with other people who lie, cheat, and steal and we come out with a clean slate. If we *do* find ourselves guilty of something, we downplay it, quickly finding someone who committed some act far worse or more notorious.

It's all a game that Self teaches us to play because it must – at every turn – cover its own weakness and faults. We must come to believe that we are wonderful people, and Self is there to lead the way to that belief.

Unfortunately, Self has nothing good for us, which is why God knows that by following Self, we not only move *away* from God, but we stand opposed to Him. Walking away from Self is the only way that pleases God because in so doing, we walk *toward* God. We cannot do this in our own strength, though, and too many people believe we can.

Salvation is the very thing that knocks Self off the throne. No longer are we interested in bragging about Self. We learn to boast only in Jesus.

Chapter 7
Self and Arrogance

Arrogance is a great deal like boasting. One stems from the other. An arrogant person thinks of him/herself first and others second (if he/she thinks of them at all). Arrogant people are often very off-putting because the stench of arrogance travels far. People who run into or have to deal with a person who is arrogant often find it annoying to the point of becoming angry.

Of course, if it turns out that your boss is the one who is arrogant, that anger must be kept in check or you risk losing your job. Arrogant people have little time for others because they are too busy thinking of themselves.

Merriam-Webster defines *arrogance* as "*an attitude of superiority manifested in an overbearing manner or in presumptuous claims or assumptions.*"[6] That is an excellent definition, isn't it?

Those who are arrogant often come across as having a superiority complex. Moreover, they tend to see and even treat other people with a form of contempt. This is because arrogant people believe they are self-made, just like those who boast.

While an arrogant person may not verbally boast about their own achievements and talents, their *attitudes* tell us everything we need to know about them. The arrogant person has a difficult time with patience, believing that the people of this world who are not as great as they (and there are many, they believe) are there for the purpose of *serving* them.

Ultimately, the arrogant person serves Self, but like others who also serve Self, doesn't realize it; so wrapped up in Self are they that they are literally blind to the presence of Self. They have unilaterally become one with Self and therefore are unable to distinguish between Self and their own personality.

What I find particularly interesting in 2 Timothy 3:2-5 is the escalation that occurs within an individual from start to finish. Here are the verses again: "*For men will be lovers of self, lovers of money, boastful, arrogant, revilers, disobedient to parents, ungrateful, unholy, unloving, irreconcilable, malicious gossips, without self-control, brutal, haters of good, treacherous, reckless, conceited, lovers of pleasure rather than lovers of God, holding to a form of godliness, although they have denied its power.*"

Notice where this transition begins in the text of Scripture. It starts with elevating Self above *all* things. Once a person begins to stare directly into the eyes of Self, the other things in Paul's list are not that

---

[6] http://www.merriam-webster.com/dictionary/arrogance (06/13/2011)

far behind. Self knows that in order to realize pleasure, money is needed. Money – and lots of it – will make things happen for Self.

As stated, it is not money in and of itself that is evil, but *loving* money inordinately is wrong. People who tend to love money elevate it as the primary purpose for living. The goal becomes gathering as much money as possible in order to be able to eat, drink, and be merry (cf. Luke 12:19). So, these folks often spend a good portion of their life working very hard to obtain as much money as possible. Their vision is that at some point, they will be able to quit working and just enjoy life.

Every year, thousands of hopefuls line up to audition for a chance to compete on *American Idol*. Why do they do this? They do it for money and fame. Very few of them come through the experience unscathed without winding up worshiping Self even more.

This is the mirage that Self creates for the person. Let's face it, a person who spends thirty or forty years or more trying to gain as much wealth as possible has created a pattern in their life. That pattern is work, work, and *more* work. Is there ever a point in their life where a person like that will come to believe they have amassed enough money to actually retire and do nothing, or only the things they want to do?

For that person, working for money has become so engrained in them that true retirement is never an option. They can never *sit down* inside themselves because they are always thinking about how to make their next buck.

Sure, they have gathered a great deal of money, and along the way, bought the things they wanted to have: cars, homes, boats, vacations, education for the kids, and all the rest. But they have never really been able to enjoy it. They have worked hard and have a good amount of things to show for it, but they are not happy.

Wealth does *not* provide inner peace or joy. It provides an endless need to gather more wealth. Look at all the rich, well-known people who are miserable. There is a connection there that we should not miss, and Paul spells it out for us in Scripture. Paul's entire list begins with loving Self so much that a person begins to love money and all the things that money can buy. From there, he moves to being boastful. It's a logical progression because a person who begins to serve Self soon realizes that the best way to serve Self comes through amassing a fortune of money. Once the money begins rolling in, the person can begin to feed Self.

Self then takes it from there with some erstwhile boasting. There is nothing quite as good as bragging about all the hard work that Self has done to cause a person to become wealthy. But people who boast or brag in Self can quickly become very arrogant. They look back over their lives and understand that they worked hard for what they gained. Instead of appreciating how much work went into that, they can begin to lose focus on the truth and start to think that they have a Midas touch, or that they are truly something to behold. The world should notice, they believe.

So, they tend to become even more focused on Self, and since Self has no room for anyone else to compete with it, it begins to see people as less than, not equal to, itself, and certainly there only to help Self gain its goals.

Arrogance in people often comes across as insincerity to others. This is because the only time an arrogant, self-made person truly needs anyone is when they realize that the person can give or get them something. When that happens, Self can pour on the charm, making others feel wonderful about themselves. People then begin to feel that they are something worthwhile to the other person who is guided by Self.

However, once Self gets what it needs/wants, it quickly goes back to its ways of focusing solely on itself. The person that they spent time puffing up is now promptly ignored. This particular trait over time is seen by many for what it is: *disingenuousness*. Because of this, the person who worships Self often has few if any true friends. No one hangs around that long because all will eventually realize that they are being used to accomplish a goal, and when that goal is accomplished, they are simply tossed aside. These people have very little feelings for anyone because their feelings are spent focusing on Self.

Chapter 8

Self and Reviling

Reviling someone is essentially a form of *hatred*. People who revile others tend to abuse them *verbally*. Why do people do this? Simply because they have grown to a point where they firmly believe they are better than the person they are denigrating. Because of this, it is their responsibility to straighten the other person out, and this is done rather caustically and even sarcastically.

Most of us can and do use sarcasm at times. It is not a good thing, except when possibly used sparingly and in a good-natured way. Sarcasm can be biting and leave emotional scars. So the person who started out desiring to become wealthy soon may become someone who boasts in his/her achievements. From there, after a time of believing their own press, they will become arrogant and will lord it over others. Arrogance will lead to abusing other people verbally and emotionally because, let's face it, those who are arrogant think primarily (and often *only*) of Self.

Self is not injured when an arrogant person reviles someone else. In fact, Self is often kept from being injured because of the injuries it perpetrates on others. Self becomes more puffed up.

If we look at Scripture, the Pharisees were often described as arrogant people, and their biting sarcasm toward the average person stung. But how did the Pharisees come to exist? Historically, during the time between the Old and New Testaments, since the Temple did not exist and therefore the sacrificial system was not practiced, a group of men came to the fore to emphasize Mosaic Law. That was not bad; however, the Pharisees actually came to interpret that law and wound up adding many additional requirements that were the epitome of absurdity.

They were often the very rich in the Jewish community and because of that alone, they were important. However, when you add to that the idea that these men interpreted Scripture and taught people how to "be saved," the level of importance really goes up.

Jesus was always arguing with them because they normally called into question many of the things that He did. He had no choice but to rebut their futile and pitiful arguments.

Jesus was not above calling their bluff, and at one point, Jesus charged that the Pharisees love all the attention they received from the average person. In Luke 11, beginning with verse forty-one, Jesus lets them have it in no uncertain terms. *"But woe to you Pharisees! For you pay tithe of mint and rue and every kind of garden herb, and yet disregard justice and the love of God; but these are the things you should have done without neglecting the others. Woe to you Pharisees! For you love the chief seats in the synagogues and the respectful greetings in the market places. Woe to you! For you are like concealed tombs, and the people who walk over them are unaware of it"* (Luke 11:41- 44). Pretty sad. According to Jesus, the Pharisees:

1. *Disregarded justice*
2. *Disregarded loving God*
3. *Love the best seats in the synagogues*
4. *Love respectful greetings*
5. *Are dead inside*

No wonder a lawyer came up to Jesus after He made these statements and told Jesus that what He said was insulting (cf. Luke 11:45), because often people did not differentiate between Pharisees and lawyers. So, Jesus told that lawyer which way was up as well. *"Woe to you lawyers as well! For you weigh men down with burdens hard to bear, while you yourselves will not even touch the burdens with one of your fingers. Woe to you! For you build the tombs of the prophets, and it was your fathers who killed them"* (Luke 11:46-47).

It would seem that the religious leaders of Jesus' day were not that great. In fact, it would appear that their arrogance kept them from actually being able to deal truthfully with people. That is certainly not uncommon.

Of course, in today's politically correct world, Jesus would have been castigated for making such statements, which would have been interpreted as "hate speech." The truth of the matter is that just after these two exchanges, both groups got together to see if they could catch Jesus in something they could charge Him with…say, *blasphemy* perhaps?

So it should be clear that *loving* money inordinately leads to boasting, arrogance, and then verbally and emotionally abusing people because they just don't have what it takes and they certainly do not come up to Self's standard.

Because of my days in acting, I have met a number of celebrities. These folks normally run in their own circles, of course. Part of that is because they want to have friends with whom they have things in common. That's not unusual and it's certainly what all of us try to do. The big difference, though, between highly-paid celebrities and the rest of us is that we normally hang out with people because we have things in common with them, not because we think we are better than others as a general rule.

Celebrities, by and large, think of themselves as better than the rest of us. They do this because

1. *They have money*
2. *They have fame*
3. *They have security*
4. *They are surrounded with people who only know how to say "yes" to everything*
5. *They tend to believe their own press*
6. *Even if/when they get in trouble with the law, they are handled differently than the average person*

In other words, rich and famous people are *privileged* in society. This was the case in Jesus' day and it is the case in our day. Privilege has its allies and plenty of perks.

But the Bible has a completely different view of rich and poor people. The Psalms and Proverbs are filled with important statements, but I think James sums up what is wrong with our society today the best. *"But the brother of humble circumstances is to glory in his high position; and the rich man is to glory in his humiliation, because like flowering grass he will pass away. For the sun rises with a scorching wind and withers the grass; and its flower falls off and the beauty of its appearance is destroyed; so too the rich man in the midst of his pursuits will fade away"* (James 1:9-11).

This is so true. The person who is poor can often be among the most humble. James does not stop with the statements above, but continues by pointing out clearly the difference between the rich and the poor. *"My brethren, do not hold your faith in our glorious Lord Jesus Christ with an attitude of personal favoritism. For if a man comes into your assembly with a gold ring and dressed in fine clothes, and there also comes in a poor man in dirty clothes, and you pay special attention to the one who is wearing the fine clothes, and say, 'You sit here in a good place,' and you say to the poor man, 'You stand over there, or sit down by my footstool,' have you not made distinctions among yourselves, and become judges with evil motives? Listen, my beloved brethren: did not God choose the poor of this world to be rich in faith and heirs of the kingdom which He promised to those who love Him? But you have dishonored the poor man. Is it not the rich who oppress you and personally drag you into court? Do they not blaspheme the fair name by which you have been called?"* (James 2:1-7).

The saddest part of what James is describing is the fact that this still happens today. Consider the mega-church that has grown so large it is ridiculous. Because of the size of that church body, there are many opportunities for everyone to get involved. There are also normally many pastors on staff. All of this takes money, and *lots* of it. Because of this, the rich person is needed; at least that's what the people of that church may think. So, once again, the rich are catered to by members and staff of that church so that they will stay and be happy, and so that they will *give*.

But look what James says about the situation. In spite of the fact that the rich are treated better even in churches, that same rich person will not hesitate to take a poor person to court if it suits them. The rich are often the ones who oppress the poor because the rich set the prices for goods and services, and too often those prices become a real stumbling block to the poor, who cannot afford it. Because they cannot afford it – their rent, for instance – the rich will take them to court to get what they believe is owed them, instead of taking into consideration the working poor that is being forced out of house and home.

The rich man can be obnoxious to a fault. Look at the rich man and Lazarus. In Luke 16:10-31, while he lived, the rich man had it all. The poor man, Lazarus, begged at the man's gate. In the afterlife, the tables were turned and it was the rich man that suffered. In spite of this, he expected Abraham to send Lazarus over to *serve* him! How arrogant can a person be?

The Pharisees spent their lives ridiculing and reviling those who were beneath them. They did not care that they were creating emotional scars. Self was securely on the throne of their lives, and because of it the worst within them was coming out.

Self can at times seem so altruistic. Yet, beneath the surface, there is a problem with Self that will not only eventually come to the fore, but will destroy the image of God within a person. By that I'm not saying that every person is automatically saved, nor am I saying that God automatically lives in every person. I'm saying that since humanity was created in God's image, that image – though marred within us – is fully salvageable through salvation. The person not availing themselves of salvation is doing Self a major favor. The more Self has to work with, the greater the damage Self does to the soul.

People who end up in hell are sent there because they *choose* to be sent there, through years or decades of listening to and following the dictates of Self. If you consider the fact that those in hell will simply spend all of eternity becoming even *more* self-centered, then we begin to understand why hell is *hell*, even apart from the torment of a constant blazing inferno attempting to purify (as fire does), but never able to accomplish that goal.

Chapter 9
Self and Disobedience

Self has unique ways of getting and keeping our attention. Self wants to be absolute, and when it is, it brings with it disappointment. The person who begins to look to Self for answers will find none. The only thing that person will find is they have chained themselves to a horrible taskmaster. Their life will be filled with unending disappointments, struggles, and unfulfilled aspirations. Even when they become successful, failure is still within reach. But Self does not care, because it has no room to care about anything but Self.

We have seen how it all starts, with a love for money. From there, the natural progression takes the person down the thorny path to unhappiness and unfulfilled dreams. At the same time, the person who has become enslaved to Self finds it impossible to break away from the binds that keep him/her firmly attached to the Self.

Not everyone who serves Self gets their wishes. For every person who makes it in business, in Hollywood, or in the music industry, for instance, thousands upon thousands do *not* make it. What's the problem? After all, they are all likely serving Self.

The problem is that there is only so much room at the top, and those who sell themselves out to forces opposed to God have a much better chance of achieving their aspirations. There is no guarantee, though. Satan couldn't care less. He picks and chooses whom he will use based on what he wants, not what the individual wants.

But if we consider the fact that we have progressed from loving *money*, to becoming *boastful*, to being full-blown *arrogant*, to then emotionally and verbally abusing people, how far is it to the next step? Disobedience is a form of arrogance because it causes individuals to believe that because they are who they are, the laws of the land do not necessarily apply to them.

I taught in the public schools for roughly ten years before moving on to teach at college, where I have been teaching since 2000. During my years as a public school teacher, I was amazed and sometimes floored at the level of verbal abuse some students would engage in with teachers, other adults, and one another. It was incredible to see these students act out the way they did, and either the parents had no control at home, or they tended to believe that their children were not as bad as all that and there was something instigating their behavior. Normally, it was either directly stated or inferred that the teacher had something to do with it. Weak administrators often caved into the parental pressure.

Every generation can be heard bemoaning how disrespectful young people are during that generation. It was no different during Jesus' day and afterwards. If I compare my generation with today's generation, my generation tends to pale in comparison, and I have already alluded to one specific example earlier having to do with leaving the fairgrounds and encountering two young men who were leaving at the same time and whose choice of verbiage did not please my father.

People today are severely disobedient, and it is not simply relegated to young people. I'm the type of person, for instance, who always uses my blinker when I drive. It is simply a habit, and I have a bumper sticker on my car that I made up for myself, which reads, "*I Use My Blinkers So You Don't Have To Guess Which Way I'm Turning.*"

Whether it's non-use of blinkers, using the cell phone while driving (without a hands free unit), cutting others off, or something else entirely, it stems from the fact that people have become severely disobedient to the laws of the land.

Even though in California it is against the law to use a cell phone while driving unless you have a hands free device hooked up to your ear, that seems not to matter to the majority of people. I routinely see people either talking on their phones or even *texting*. The reason people don't follow the law is because it is *inconvenient* for them to do so.

To use your cell phone legally while driving in California means having to purchase an extra Bluetooth wireless device or some type of speaker system. That is an expense that many prefer not to have to indulge in, so it's easier to break the law. Never mind that it affects safety on the highways.

Not using your car blinkers is actually also breaking the law, but few ever get ticketed for it. For many, rather than being seen as a law, it is simply seen as how much of a convenience or not it is to use the blinker. In other words, it is a *suggestion*.

Some argue that when they use their blinker to try to change lanes, people in that lane speed up so they cannot squeeze into that lane. Others argue that if no one is behind them, they see no need to use it.

The trouble is that if a person gets into the routine of using their blinkers at all times, it will simply become a habit and, therefore, will not be inconvenient because it won't even register when using it. It will simply be automatic.

Think of all the laws that people break during any given day: seemingly harmless laws, but they are broken nonetheless. Speeding is a big problem, and most of us go over the speed limit. Part of the problem is that to go the actual speed limit means going slower than just about every other car on the road. Law enforcement knows this, which is why they generally look for the person who is going even faster than most or driving recklessly, changing lanes while speeding, weaving in and out, or even going the speed limit in the car pool lane while the cars in the other lanes next to the car pool lane are stopped or going very slowly. You're traveling the speed limit or faster in the car pool lane and some impatient person from the next lane over pulls into the car pool lane because they're tired of going slow or being stopped. What they've done is illegal, but because you are driving so fast, there is a good likelihood that you will crash into the back of them.

The reality with bad drivers is that they drive the way they drive because they simply do not care about other people. They are disobedient to the laws of the land because it suits them to be so.

Young people are no different, and unfortunately, like all of us, they develop their bad habits of lawlessness by watching their parents and other adults. It's called hypocrisy when we try to tell someone to do something that we ourselves do not do.

It isn't long before these same young people begin to act out against their parents. They see their parents as being duplicitous or hypocritical and therefore have lost authority.

Many teens today have taken an approach where their parents are concerned that completely eliminates those parents from their lives. They don't care about their parents; they have their own lives, and they live them. For the parents' part, they either throw their hands up in defeat, or wrongly believe that Johnny or Janie is simply going through a phase, which will pass.

Disobedience is a huge problem in society. The most frustrating part about it is when some gangbanger gets into trouble and winds up in a police shootout, forcing the police to end his life. Normally, the parents are the first ones who claim that little Johnny was an angel and got along with everyone. How could the police take their young son's life like that?

Well, that young man's life was taken because he was doing something that warranted police involvement. Instead of obeying the police when they caught up to him, he chose to barricade himself in a house and then try to shoot his way to safety.

It doesn't take long for a kid who has become disobedient to parents to get to the point where listening to or obeying other people in authority are treated the same way. This is the logical progression of the person who begins wholeheartedly catering to Self. Before he/she realizes it, everything in life is measured against the desires of Self and anything that does not coincide with Self is tossed out, including obedience to authority.

There is a natural tendency among people to balk at having to respond positively to people in authority. We don't like being told what to do, how to do it, where we can do it, and when it can be done. We just do not like it because it *chafes* us. It's like a large splinter under a fingernail. It just doesn't feel good, so we tend to rebel, or kick against the goads, as the Bible says. Paul, in telling us about his conversion in the book of Acts (cf. Acts 9:5; 26:14), mentions this metaphor. "*Ultimately, 'kick against the goads' is a metaphor. Goads were used to prod cattle and livestock forward, and they would frequently kick back at them, only causing themselves more injury. The thought is that Paul has been kicking against God's 'goading,' and God has been trying to urge him to go in a certain direction.*"[7]

People who kick against the goads are literally rebelling, whether it's against parents, police officers, or God Himself. We all have tendencies to do this, simply because even Christians still have Self within and must spend the remainder of their lives fighting against its wants and desires.

As our two kids grew up, my wife and I tried our best to bring them up in a way that involved loving them immensely. Don't be misled, though, because that love involved discipline too. It is sometimes difficult to know how to best apply the necessary form of discipline because the last thing you want to do is make them feel as though you are *reviling* them, which destroys them emotionally, or at least creates scars. At the same time, they need to understand the full import of their misdeeds. It is a constant balancing act that cannot simply be read about in some book somewhere. It takes God's grace, strength, and love to be a good parent. We are *never* perfect at it.

Our children are both adults now, and I think it is safe to say that both our kids really love us. Moreover, they actually *enjoy* being with us, yet they have their own friends too, and their own lives.

---

[7] http://wiki.answers.com/Q/In_the_Bible_what_does_to_'kick_against_the_goads'_mean#ixzz1PCNbZ78c

We have fun together, but we have not worried about trying to be their *friend*. We have always been their parents since the day they were born, but we have tried hard to enter into their lives, to be there for them, to love them as much as we can, and to discipline them when they stray. God does the same for us, and our prayer has always been that *we* will discipline them as *He* disciplines us.

Too many parents (in my opinion, not that I'm an expert) really do not know how to raise their kids with the proper use of discipline. I'm not talking about beating the living daylights out of them. I'm talking about helping them to understand consequences, and sometimes that takes a particularly firm and even somewhat angry voice to do it.

When our kids were babies, starting to crawl around, we made sure that we had – to the best of our ability – made the house child-proof. You can't make a house perfectly child-proof, but there is a great deal you can do. Plugging up open outlets, putting soft rubber tips on corners of sharp counters, etc., help the child remain safe.

Sometimes, though, in spite of how well a parent tries to child-proof the house, the child will still find a way to create a problem for him/herself. If I saw my child getting ready to stick something in an outlet that was uncovered, I would probably slap their hand quickly. It wouldn't be enough to leave a mark or cause great pain, but it would be enough to get their attention and let them know that doing what they were about to do will cause pain anyway. Chances are great that they will not do that again.

Too many parents will simply take the child aside and "talk" to that child in a very soothing voice about why they shouldn't stick anything in an open outlet. Well, of course, the problem is that this is not age-appropriate discipline for that child. If they are barely a toddler, they don't understand your words and the soothing tone of voice may even confuse them into thinking they were doing nothing wrong, but that you simply wanted to come over and make them feel warm and gushy inside.

I've seen cases of parents knocking their kids around for the slightest infraction, or pretty much letting them do what they want to do. In both cases, a disobedient child can be created from those actions.

Disobedience is not a pretty attribute in anyone, but it is a growing one in our global society. Lately, we have seen the fall of Tunisia, Egypt, and Libya (currently ongoing), as well as many protests in Saudi Arabia, Bahrain and too many places to list. The attitude of much of the world is that they don't have to listen to anyone anymore. They can make their own laws.

I'm *not* saying that a person should knuckle under and cater to the inordinate demands of a dictator. But generally, in our society today people feel much more emboldened to *disobey* those in authority rather than obey them.

This much is true. The logical progression of Paul's list to Timothy is definitely on display today. Instead of wanting peace in the world or their local society, people would rather stand up for individual rights, even if they are wrong. When I say *wrong*, I'm basing my opinion of what is right and wrong on what the Bible teaches.

Just recently, one particular Gay group has started a petition drive to force the Southern Baptist Convention to apologize for the way it characterizes homosexuality as sin. They complain that this is doing irreparable harm to them and their lifestyle.

The reality is that either the Bible teaches that homosexuality is wrong or it is not. Obviously, homosexual groups argue that the teaching of Scripture is being misunderstood and misrepresented, or they charge that Jesus never spoke against homosexuality. That's their opinion, but their opinion does not negate the opinion of other people who believe that homosexuality is a sin in the Bible, just like adultery, fornication, stealing, and more are considered sinful.

No one that I'm aware of in the United States (except for possibly one ultra-fringe group) wants homosexuals *dead*. Because homosexuals take umbrage at those who believe and teach that the Bible indicates that homosexuality is a sinful practice is no reason for people to apologize for it.

Gay groups will not stop until negative statements against homosexuality are seen as hate-crimes and treated as criminal offenses. So, in effect, these Gay rights groups have become the *wordsmith* police. They do not want anyone to offer their opinion *against* the Gay lifestyle, and moreover, they want those people who do to be ticketed or arrested. The apostle Paul, under those conditions, would have been imprisoned (cf. Romans 1-2).

This all stems from the fact that people are not content to simply live their lives the way they see fit. They believe they have to make laws that protect them from *hearing* comments that denigrate their lifestyle. How absurd is this? Is there any other area in society in which hate-crimes can be stamped on a person for offering their biblical opinion?

Disobedience to parents and all forms of authority generate from Self. Those people who cater to Self eventually come to see their life as more important than anyone else's, and because of that, every effort should be made to prop themselves up.

This is a real slippery slope. I recall driving through San Francisco one afternoon with my son. While stopped at a traffic light, a man in a bright blue tutu and heels waltzed past us in the crosswalk. To me, it was unintentionally one of the funniest things I've seen, but that wasn't the funniest part. The funniest part was noticing the look on the city bus driver's face only a few lanes over who stared at the same tutu man as if he had never seen anything quite like it. This was from an employee of the city of San Francisco, who likely thought he had seen everything.

Out of courtesy for the man in the tutu, I stifled my laugh. I have to say that it was terribly difficult to keep my laughter in check, though. To see this tall, thin man, with hairy legs, a tutu, heels, a five o'clock shadow, and mustache walk in front of my car in the crosswalk was almost too much for me. Had I been drinking something, I'm sure it would have found its way out of my mouth, through my nose, and onto the dashboard and windshield.

What else can we possibly assume when we see people demanding that the rest of the world not only accepts their lifestyle, but must also refrain from reacting to it in such a way that may cause them embarrassment? We can only assume that Self is on the throne in a mighty big way. Everywhere we look in society, we see demands of Self attempting to gain more inroads.

Whether it's people who refuse to use Bluetooth wireless devices for their phones while driving, not using a blinker because it's just too inconvenient, or demanding that the rest of the world shut up and like another person's lifestyle because that's the way they choose to live, it all comes from the same source: Self.

Ultimately, the dictates of *Self* lead only to *anarchy*.

Chapter 10

Self and Ungratefulness

L ike many things, being *ungrateful* is often seen in a person's attitude and demeanor. Ungrateful people are fairly easy to spot. They simply lack the good sense to appreciate what they have, and they also unfortunately have come to believe that what they have is *deserved* and that they never quite get all that they fully merit.

This way of thinking is closely tied to being arrogant and boastful, yet it *is* beyond both. People who are ungrateful have gone past boasting and arrogance and have arrived to the point where they somehow believe that they have been shortchanged in life. This thinking leads them to become soured at the least and angry to bitter at worst. Ungrateful people will always manage to bring the conversation back to them and do so in a way that makes other people feel very uncomfortable. They simply cannot understand why the world has not noticed them and heaped praise and gifts on them at every turn.

Ungrateful people often become very jaded and have long gone past the ability to see and appreciate any good things that might come their way. Oh, to be sure, they may genuinely appreciate things – for a very short period of time. However, in short order, this gives way to the belief that they did not receive *all* they were due.

If you have ever been around someone with a personality disorder, this becomes quite clear. For instance, a person with, say, Borderline Personality Disorder or Narcissistic Personality Disorder believes most of the time that people simply do not treat them with the respect and honor they deserve.

People like this tend to see the world in black and white, with no gray areas. Either you are *for* them, or you are *against* them. You're either the person they love, or the person they hate. There is no in-between with folks like this, so it is better to understand right from the start that they are what they are and it has nothing to do with you. You just happen to be in the line of fire at the time.

The real tragedy here is that people like this do not see themselves *as* what I've described. They see themselves as truly loving people, yet they are always disappointed with *other people* because of the expectations they place on them. While they see themselves as loving unconditionally and always ready to forgive, the truth is that they can keep lists of infractions (real and perceived) against others a mile long. When things go bad, they have no hesitation in referencing that list of theirs.

It really does not matter what you do *for* them, but it certainly matters what you do *to* them (or what *they* perceive you do to them). These events become mountains that are virtually walls that do not allow forward movement. They stand in the way of progressing, and that is due to the fact that people like this *cannot* let things go, though they firmly believe they can and do. The fact that they can throw past infractions up as quickly as they do disproves their own belief.

The problem is exacerbated because everything is perceived by them as some huge problem that *you* created. Yes, it's your fault. Everything you did created the problem. They were simply the innocent bystanders and victims of your self-centeredness, and now they are left to simply *respond*.

The real truth of the matter is that every one of us makes mistakes. We all sin, even those people who do not believe they do sin. When those folks start looking at you as if *your* sins are bigger or worse than *their* sins are, at that point it is likely that you will find yourself on the receiving end of their ire, often unbridled.

You see, the *ungrateful* person has found a way to hammer home to you or anyone who will listen how badly you (or someone else) have treated them. They will complain about everything, and nothing is ever good enough for them.

Think about people in your life. Have you ever had to deal with someone like this? It is not fun, is it, and in fact, it can drive you crazy until you realize that it really is *not* your fault. It has everything to do with the way they comprehend life. Yes, you are human. Yes, you may have inadvertently done some things that have caused others pain here and there, but you know yourself. You know you're not heartless. You *know* that you did not do all the things they said you did.

Once you begin to see this with clarity, you realize that for however long you were in any type of relationship with a person that I've been describing, you were hoodwinked. You were blinded to the fact that you were abused emotionally. You always thought it was *your* fault! Now, you have come to realize that *they* pushed the issue. They worked hard to make you feel that you could never thoroughly please them. They even managed to question your love for them or your loyalty to them, or something else, repeatedly.

You have finally come to terms with the fact that you were in relationship with someone – a friend, a family member, a spouse – who blamed you at every turn, and while you *know* you were not perfect, it was very difficult to see yourself in the way *they* saw you. You were just not that person, and it caused tremendous stress on you.

This is how the ungrateful person lives and works. Think about the relationships you *know* that person had over the years. How were things for them at work? Did they constantly complain about people at work and how they always felt as if they were not respected as they "should" have been? Did their employment always end badly with them feeling relieved to leave, as if leaving *that* job was the end of their problems, only to have repeats regardless of where they worked from that point onward?

In other words, the job didn't matter. It was the *people*. For some reason, they were always downtrodden and underappreciated. They were always being picked on for no known reason, and you even came to believe, as they did, that their life was cursed. They told you and the proof was seen in their life, so it must be true, right?

People who are ungrateful do not have an accurate picture or understanding of life in general. They are completely unable to deal with life head-on, and they seem to be forever stuck in this rut of having to learn the same things over and over again because they never progress beyond those things.

I know a person who made statements like this (due to how miserable her life was):

- *Oh, when I see God [in the afterlife], He and I are going to sit down for a very long talk.*
- *I understand what Job went through.*
- *Why does God hate me?*
- *Satan has wanted to destroy me.*

These and other statements are presented *genuinely*. That person truly believes that he/she is equal to Job in the amount of suffering they have experienced in their life, yet all of their suffering, for the most part, has been *emotional* suffering based on their faulty thinking and perspective.

Job's suffering, on the other hand, was mainly physical, and at times extremely painful, and always perplexing. In all of that, he never blasphemed God. He continued to submit himself to God, even though he got to a point of being annoyed at his situation and even felt a bit sorry for himself. Who can blame him? I can't. Can you?

Imagine, though, making a statement like the first bullet. Wow, talk about demagoguery. The individual making that comment was saying that he/she knew better than God and that in fact, God *owed* him/her a full explanation of everything. That type of thinking is extremely dangerous for anyone, much less someone who claims to be a Christian. It is the height of Self's desires.

In those four statements, we see – in each one of them – a form of pride that has created the false perception that the person is extremely important. In fact, they obviously believe that they are so important that Satan wants nothing more than to destroy him/her. Why *that* person and not others? In point of fact, Satan would destroy *all* people, especially Christians, if given the opportunity to do so.

Ungrateful people are often an enigma to the rest of us. That is not to say that all people in general do not go through times of slight depression, or simply feeling as though God has turned a deaf ear to their pleas. I'm talking about people who live their lives in such a way that they wind up constantly comparing their perceived situation with other people, and they always come up wanting.

Ungrateful people are often extremely *insecure*. It is normally because of this that these folks must do whatever they can to *be* and *remain* in the spotlight. They cannot be left out of the conversation, and in short order they will become the center of that conversation. If allowed, they will direct the discussion to include aspects of their life, their goals, their aspirations and dreams, and they expect everyone to listen with bated breath.

Ungrateful people can be severely off-putting and that adds to their feelings of ungratefulness. They obviously do not see themselves as ungrateful at all, so they naturally wonder why people do not like them that much. In fact, if pushed, they will say that they are extremely giving and loving. Because of that, they wonder why they have wound up hurt as often as they have been.

It makes sense that the person who has become ungrateful (regardless of the road they took to arrive there) has become extremely selfish. The more selfish they become, they less they see themselves as selfish. This is because Self does everything it can to hide that fact from that person by creating false impressions that satisfy the *ego*.

In fact, Self does what it can to hide that fact from all of us. It needs to do so in order to continue to be the king on the throne. Once the Holy Spirit enters (with salvation) and begins to work in the life of the authentic Christian, Self's hiding places are routed out and we begin to see what we are actually like as God sees us. The Holy Spirit, of course, has a very gentle, non-threatening way of allowing us to see the reality of our lives. His goal is to help us move away from being like that, not to condemn us because of it.

We are all selfish to some extent. The person who has become ungrateful through the years is essentially moving away from God, regardless of what they think they are doing. This is obviously the case, because the ungrateful person who is adamantly and routinely ungrateful is focused solely on Self, yet does not see it.

If you have someone in your life that you know to be thoroughly ungrateful, your job is to *pray* for them, that God will slowly begin to open their eyes and shift their gaze away from Self. This is the best way that you can love them. You can also do yourself a huge favor and realize that you are *not* to blame for the way they feel. You can refuse to give ear to *their* perceptions as if those perceptions are truth, when they are really little more than emotional harpoons directed at you.

God loves you and He loves them exactly the same way. Just as He wants *you* free from their emotional control and abuse, He wants *them* free from their own hallowed view of Self. You can help them get there by no longer enabling them and praying for them without ever ceasing. Their soul may depend upon it.

Chapter 11
Self and Unholiness

In a nutshell, holiness is when someone is separated *to* God. People who become authentic Christians begin the process of moving away from the world and its influences and closer to God through greater devotion to Him coupled with a willingness to follow Him more completely. Opposite this stands *unholiness*, which is literally the state of being completely separated *from* God. We are born into the world this way because of the fact that we are born in sin. Remaining in sin *keeps* us unholy. The tragic part is that though people often believe they have found something that brings them *closer* to God in communion and fellowship, instead they have simply found a way to remain apart from God, continuing to be unholy, but deceived into thinking that they are on their way to becoming holy. There are many practices today, which can keep us from God in unholiness, all the while convincing us that we are on the path leading *to* God.

We've all heard the phrases *astral projection* or *out of body experience* (or *OOBE*). When we hear them we think of individuals who go into something like a trance where their consciousness separates physically from their body, yet it is still connected through what is termed the "silver cord." In that situation, the silver cord is the only thing that keeps a person's conscious awareness connected to their physical body. To sever or destroy that silver cord means to kill the person's physical body.

As I have begun to study this area called astral projection, I cannot help but realize the dangers and full evil potential of the spiritual entities that wait just on the other side of our own physical dimension for opportunities that we may provide them, either intentionally or unintentionally. However, to actively participate in what is known as astral projection, in nearly all respects, a person must want to go there. This is not always the case, but in order for astral projection to occur, something must be generated so that a combination of brain waves together will cause this separation, or altered state of consciousness.

I was recently listening to an audio broadcast by Russ Dizdar (*The Black Awakening*) where he related his understanding of astral projection, along with the dangers of it and how he has helped people break free of its hold on them. During the broadcast, he discussed the craze of astral sex and its effects on people's lives. He also talked of many of the resources both on the Internet and in books that have helped him realize just how involved with this area so many people have become.

One Web site states, "*Using brainwave technology it was found that a certain combination of alpha and theta harmonics caused the immediate transference of consciousness away from the physical body.*"[8] There are even places on the Internet where audio CDs can be purchased that create this type of separation after listening to the audio for twenty minutes or so through headphones.

People involved in this practice of astral projection often speak of the amazing things they see and experience. They also describe their bodies almost as if they were like a type of Jell-O, yet able to control that astral body's movements with practice. There are many instances of people sharing examples of what happens to them during these times of out-of-body experiences and even astral projection sex that can and often happens.

Many to most of these people are not aware of the types of entities and beings they are dealing with in that disconnected state of mind. What I think we fail to realize is that we exist presently within three dimensions (four, if you count time as one of those dimensions). It seems to me that since the fall of humanity, God has made it so that we are sequestered to these dimensions, yet we want to experience more. We are not supposed to try to leave these dimensions for any other dimensions that exist.

The truth of the matter is that any dimensions beyond the dimensions in which we currently live without question are dimensions where spiritual entities and beings exist. While their own home base is outside of my four dimensions, they can obviously come into and leave my dimensions as they will. They can and do affect the lives of people in the here and now. The many instances of demonic possession and control of circumstances throughout the Bible bear this out clearly.

---

[8] http://oobe.mind-sync.com/newage/artastralastralprojectionsex.html

Think about it for a moment. In the Bible, we know that certain prophets and apostles were actually allowed to leave their bodies for short periods of time, allowing them to see and to some extent even experience the events of the future. We read of some of these events throughout Ezekiel or the book of Revelation, and though Ezekiel or John speak of seeing something *"in the Spirit,"* it is clear that God was the one who – for that specific purpose – allowed them to leave their bodies through a vision or something similar, for one purpose: to learn what would happen in the future from their point in time. God did this so that generations to come would know what God had planned. As these prophecies spoken of by Ezekiel, John, and others came to pass, it also becomes clear that the veracity of the Bible is, once again, upheld.

In 2 Thessalonians 2, Paul speaks of how the final world dictator known as the man of sin (or the Antichrist) will become known, mostly due to the fact that the world itself will have become so perverse in the last days. Paul tells us that this man of sin's *"coming is in accord with the activity of Satan, with all power and signs and false wonders, and* **with all the deception of wickedness for those who perish**, *because they did not receive the love of the truth so as to be saved"* (2 Thessalonians 2:9-10; emphasis added). These counterfeit signs and miracles, along with the constant and consistent rise in today's moral perversions and addictions that do nothing but darken human understanding, are going to be clearly part of the End Times deception that he references.

Consider the exponential growth of interest in astral projection in the past few decades. Sexual activity within the realm of astral projection, or out-of-body experiences, has also grown with it. The reason for this is because it is often seen as literally having safe sex! Think about it. If a person enters into an out-of-body state through astral projection and meets beings or entities while there who start to have sex with that human person, what can happen? Can the person become pregnant (if a woman)? Can a sexually transmitted disease spread from the spiritual entity to the human being?

From my own study of the material that exists on astral projection and sex during that state, pregnancy seems to be impossible. One person put it bluntly, "*You can't get pregnant by having astral sex any more than by not having sex at all.*"[9] So the draw for people to enter into an out-of-body experience seems to rest, to some degree, in the sexual encounters they embrace during those astral events. The dangers only *seem* non-existent, but are they?

We all know that Genesis 6 tells us of the Nephilim that were created due to the fact that the fathers of those Nephilim, whom we call fallen angels, found some way to impregnate human women. We also believe that this was done purely by Satan to destroy the human strain of DNA. If the human strain of DNA was fully destroyed, there would be no chance that God would be able to enter humanity as a human being Himself (while *retaining* His full deity) in order to become the atonement for sinful humanity, thereby being able to offer salvation to the fallen race of human beings.

Both Peter and Jude allude to the fact that these particular angels (the fathers of the Nephilim) were chained in darkness by God because of their crimes of not keeping their "first estate." Jude tells us, "*And angels who did not keep their own domain, but abandoned their proper abode, He has kept in eternal bonds under darkness for the judgment of the great day*" (Jude 6). Obviously, Jude cannot be referring to *all* angels who literally fell from grace by following Satan in his rebellion against God. If so, all fallen angels would have been locked up, and we know that is not the case. Jude is speaking of *specific* angels who did something so horrendous that it caused God to lock those specific angels away until their judgment so that they

---

[9] www.starseeds.net/group/earthdragons/forum/.../sex-magick-ascension-for

could not perpetrate that same type of terribly evil sin against humanity again.

If you believe that Genesis 6 refers to the line of Seth, or some other human lineage, that's up to you. Debating with me about it isn't going to bring anyone any closer to the actual truth. If I'm wrong, then I submit myself to the Lord, who will straighten me out on that score. I'll let you do the same.

So if this was the case then during the time of Genesis 6, what is the deal now with all the talk about sexual relations in the spiritual realm during astral projection? What is the purpose of that? I believe that unlike the incidence of Genesis 6, in which God saw how terribly evil the entirety of humanity had become, except for Noah and his immediate family, today's demons are more interested in controlling humanity through direct intervention than impregnating human women.

It is quite possible that the fallen angels who found a way to have sexual intercourse with human women (and interestingly, the very book quoted by Jude [and Peter] above, called *The Book of Enoch*, refers to these beings as *The Watchers*) were different from the other angels in heaven, which is why Jesus could rightly and accurately state that the angels *in heaven* (at the time He made the statement) are neither married or given in marriage (cf. Matthew 22:30; Mark 12:25). The Watchers and the angels who fell are no longer in heaven. They may have started there, but no longer exist there. When Jesus made the statement He made, the fallen angels had long ago fallen from their original state in heaven. Specifically, if *The Book of Enoch* has any authenticity to it (and certainly both Peter and Jude believed it did enough to quote from it), these Watchers seemed to be a completely different bunch of angelic beings from Gabriel, Michael and the others. Then again, we do not know a great deal about angels in the first place, do we?

In today's world, based on 2 Thessalonians 2, it seems clear that demons and Satan want more than anything to have control over humanity. That's a given. Getting human women pregnant isn't really that fruitful. Sure, if it could happen today with demons (the spirits of the Nephilim whose physical bodies died in the flood), the result would be some hybrid that will have far greater powers and abilities than any human, yet still have less power and abilities than their spiritual fathers. They would also be inferior to the original Nephilim as well.

Paul confirms that during these last days (like all times since Creation), prior to the revelation of the man of sin, the activities of Satan are seen within his power to deceive. Satan has always deceived and he deceives in many ways. In all of those ways, he deceives through the temptation toward wickedness. I think Paul is also stating that compared to any other time in human history, this period of time leading immediately up to the Tribulation will include some of the worst and most powerful deceptions known to humanity.

Consider the false signs and especially the wonders that happen because of Satan's power with human beings *now*. Whether astral projection is true or whether it is simply an extremely strong delusion is difficult to know. However, there is a far greater abundance of people literally clamoring after these types of things because of what they (or what Self) seem to gain from their involvement in it! At the very least, it caters to the Self-centeredness of the world today!

Imagine going into an altered state of consciousness that allows a person to visit past lives or experience remote image viewing (when a person is in one place, but can see things that happen far away). During this event, a sexual encounter might be experienced. The people that tell of having these experiences speak of the intensity that overshadows anything like it in this physical realm. In other words, these people talk of emotions, urges, and feelings that are so intense they are difficult to explain and unlike anything experienced in this dimension. It is as if their astral body has become electrically charged, and because of that, all experiences, including sexual activity, become tremendously magnified.

So, we have a greater number of people seeking and even experiencing these types of events, and they can easily become addicted to them. Because of this growing addiction, they will seek them out more and more simply because of the quality of the experience itself, along with the belief that no harm can actually come from them.

One individual named *Sapphire* attests to the fact that for over 15 years she has experienced astral projection daily and has enjoyed many sexual experiences within that realm of altered consciousness. Another woman, in describing her *first* instance of astral projection, noted that while in her altered state, she first had sex with one entity, which was then followed by more encounters with numerous beings at the same time. This is nothing more than group sex – an orgy – yet since it was done in another dimension via astral projection people see nothing wrong with it. While it is real, in essence, it is not real, as far as our dimensions are concerned. It is like *dreaming*, yet dreaming vividly. Who can be held responsible for what they dream, right? Wrong.

At one point, after this woman had sex with multiple entities, she started coming back to her home, in this dimension. She began to "wake up" after she got home, and as she did, she felt the presence of yet another entity. She realized that she was not yet fully awake from her astral projection.

All of a sudden, she was on the couch, having sex with yet *another* being. This is the way she describes it: *"Next thing I knew I was on my couch, making love again, but I could only see bits of ceiling and the room as I tried to swing that tunnel vision toward the being I was with. His head was on my chest and I touched his hair and thought, "It's G [my husband at the time]." I felt like it was G, and therefore felt fine making love to him, but then I had the thought that it was a trick, and whoever it was was just making me think it was G so I'd make love to him. (I wasn't really too concerned with who it was, but was happy to think it was my husband)."*[10]

So the woman describes literally being raped by numerous entities from other dimensions, arriving back home to her couch and then being raped (though she calls it "making love") again by still a different entity who seemed to pretend to be her husband. She then notes that she began considering it was possibly a trick to make her believe it was her husband. She realized it was not. However, she deliberately chose to believe that it *was* her husband because if it was her husband, she didn't have to feel guilty about having sex.

So think of it. If people in greater numbers are involving themselves in out-of-body experiences, they will very likely become extremely addicted to these sexual events. If you consider the fact that people – by and large – seem unable to get enough sexual stimulation in this life, whether through movies, magazines, Internet porn sites, and the like, this then is just one more facet that creates an allegedly far greater sexual response than simply having physical sex with another human being in this physical realm!

People who have addictions find them extremely difficult to break. I myself have one and it has to do with *sugar*. I find myself eating candy, cookies, ice cream, or cake simply because those items are there, not necessarily because I want to eat them. I have tried many things to eliminate the cravings (including not buying sweets!) and I have had some success, but the way some people love bread, I continue to love sweets.

---

[10] http://www.muse-net.com/apsex.html

Imagine if I could go to a place where everything was sweeter and far more satisfying to my mouth and stomach than the sweets that I eat in this realm. It reminds me of *The Lion, the Witch, and the Wardrobe* when Edmund meets the White Witch and is tempted with Turkish Delight. He loves it and not getting enough of it makes him ornery. We all have weaknesses, and when they are not fulfilled, we, too, can become ornery.

In Genesis 6, I think about the possibility that Satan went to the leader of the Watchers (*The Book of Enoch*) and tempted him to lust after human women. That leader took the bait and went back to the other Watchers and, as their leader, tempted them to join him in his sin. They did, and from that horrible union of women and fallen angels the world got the Nephilim. Why did Satan tempt them to commit this terrible evil? As stated, it was to destroy the human genome so that Jesus would not be born.

Today, we have Satan and demons finding ways to cash in on the weaknesses and pleasures of human beings. Sexual relations in the proper, biblical context are, of course, fine. However, because of this deceptive manipulation, people are entering into a new frontier of uncharted sexual territory combined with demonic evil. It is leaving these people guilt-free while giving them levels of tremendous pleasure that they have not experienced before in this dimension.

In today's world – the last days of human history prior to the Tribulation – Satan does not need to actually impregnate human women so they can give birth to hybrids. What's the point of that? He doesn't need to destroy the human genome again. He already tried that and like everything else he does, he failed. He may simply choose to impregnate *one* woman with his seed in order to bring forth the Antichrist. If that's what he chose to do, then I believe he's already done that, because I believe the Antichrist already lives among us.

So why are Satan and his demonic minions involved in deceitfully engaging human beings (both women *and* men) in things like astral projection and astral sex? Simply because it opens the doors to the demonic realm, which are extremely difficult to close, and it is done so by the human being – willingly.

The person who opens that door is "rewarded" with sexual involvement that makes what they have in this realm pale in comparison in most cases. I also believe that this is simply another way that Satan tries desperately to imitate God. Let me explain.

We know that the Holy Spirit works *in* and *through* the Church. Each member of the authentic Church is indwelt by the Holy Spirit. We are empowered to overcome sin and He also works within us to change us into the image of Jesus, God the Son. For the authentic Christian who lives to serve the only wise God, our Savior, the benefits are fully realized in the next life; however, while here in this life and within our four dimensions, we still gain quite a lot. We learn what joy is, not just happiness. We begin to comprehend what God's love is all about and we come to terms with what it means to be fully forgiven. We begin to see the scope of salvation as it presents itself to us for all eternity. There are so many things that come with being an authentic believer in Jesus, words cannot describe them all.

Once the Church is gone, to a large degree the Holy Spirit's work in this world will be severely curtailed, at least initially, until He starts building things up again through the 144,000 of Revelation and their evangelistic assault on this earth, Satan's temporary kingdom. This does *not* mean that the Holy Spirit has somehow lost power. He has *not*. It is just that the largest vehicle He has deliberately chosen to work through will no longer be here.

Without the Holy Spirit, the Christian's work would amount to nothing. Because of the Holy Spirit working in and through each Christian, lives are eternally changed and God is fully magnified.

Satan works the same way, except on an evil scale. He wants and needs to work in and through people in order to fully accomplish his goals. As things ramp up toward the end and the Church is taken out of the way, the doors will be thrust open by Satan and his hordes to fully extend his evil to the world, and it will be done largely through the people they have come to control.

Those who have opened the door to what appears to be harmless sexual activity in another dimension will find themselves overpowered by demons who have merely used sex as the carrot that gave them access to the heart of the individual. Can you imagine a world in which millions of people, through one form or another, will have willingly volunteered to enjoy what seemed to be harmless pleasures for a season, only to realize later that they unknowingly gave Satan full permission to use them however he wishes to do so?

What seems to so many to be so innocuous is willingly opening the door to untold levels of evil that will force their way into this world and will quickly create the environment and atmosphere that will ultimately cater to and deliver the man of sin described in 2 Thessalonians 2 to the world. People who open the door to other dimensions do so to their own (and the world's) tremendous peril. Satan and his demons not only look for, but work to create, open doors through which they can march in order to gain control.

The person who believes that they control the situation during astral projection is fully deceived. They are led away by the pleasure they encounter and that becomes the magnet for them to return, willingly submitting themselves to experiences that we are not supposed to experience! In this case, it is what is known as Incubus/Succubus, which is the physical intermingling of human and demonic. This world is heading toward destruction simply because it is playing with dynamite that for now seems pleasurable, but the consequences for many will be nothing short of *eternal* death. What could be more *unholy* than that?

Chapter 12
Self in Politics

Self can be a potent cocktail. The desire of many who wind up serving Self tends to be *inward,* as we have mentioned throughout this book. One of the biggest ways that Self exercises its power over the individual (aside from those areas already mentioned) is through the desire to simply have fun in life.

There is nothing wrong with taking a vacation or enjoying a night out with your spouse. There is also nothing wrong with enjoying the things that life has to offer. The problem comes in when this is the perceived primary reason for our existence. People live to play.

They want to have the best TV, the coolest looking car and clothes to match.

People want to go the lake or fly to Hawaii or some other tropical paradise. They want to head to Las Vegas for a weekend of gambling, fun, and frolic.

In many cities, Friday night arrives, and people are ready to party. They take their nap in the afternoon or early evening after work and get ready for a night of debauchery and playtime. Wherever it leads is great as long as they have fun getting there. They have no real plans except to hang with their buds and go door to door, from one bar to the next.

The reality is that this type of living takes its toll, but this is the type of living that Self demands because Self endeavors to feel good about itself.

In my area of the world, there are lakes to which people who own boats flock. It is not uncommon to see trucks pulling large boats on the weekends as they head up the mountains or to the nearest lake for a day or weekend of fun and relaxation.

People today have become enamored with doing things that allow them to simply enjoy life. That's their biggest goal. We have become a people who – as Paul says – are lovers of pleasure rather than lovers of God. To many today, there is far more to gain from a day of boating, fishing, or going to the movies than from studying His Word and worshiping with other believers.

If we stop to think about the terrible shape our economy is in, we are led to believe that if we just don't think about it, it will get better. We believe our problems will just go away if we don't worry about or deal with them. Isn't that what the people in Washington DC are supposed to do? Isn't that why we voted them into office in the first place? We like to think so, but the problem, of course, is that there are far more individuals who go to Washington with a *liberal* agenda. Some go there wanting to change things for the better; however, their view of what is better is often not in line with God's view. That doesn't matter to them, because they are on their own crusade.

In the political arena, Self is very evident in politics. There are generally two groups in Washington, *liberals* and *conservatives,* and neither usually sides with the other. This can and has created gridlock often. In the state of California, for instance, I can't remember a year when the budget was actually turned in *on time.* Both Dems and Repubs sit across from one another unwilling to move *toward* one another to accomplish something for the state of California.

If you ask conservatives what the problem is, they will tell you they cannot agree with liberals who simply see raising taxes as a way to solve the budget mess. If you ask liberals what the problem is, they will say that they are tired of conservatives who only want to fund their pet projects.

This is one of the difficulties with people in politics. They often go into that arena for a variety of reasons, but many of them are downright selfish.

For instance, Congresswoman Carolyn McCarthy of New York, whose husband was shot and killed in 1993 by a deranged gunman on a commuter train, got involved in politics for that reason. Since then, she has introduced legislation to prohibit the manufacture and sale of high-capacity magazines. Beyond this, her main goal is to push for more gun control laws. Whether that's right or wrong is not the issue. The issue is *why* individuals get involved in the political arena.

We often tell ourselves that the reason we get involved is because we want to make the world a better place. That's way too altruistic these days. Usually, it has more to do with some form of catering to Self.

In the case of Carolyn McCarthy, she comes from a state where gun laws are extremely rigid and specific. In McCarthy's case, a lunatic by the name of Colin Ferguson opened fire on a commuter train in 1993, tragically killing McCarthy's husband and wounding her son.

As it turns out, Ferguson purchased the gun legally while living in California, and after waiting the 15-day time period, took the gun home. He began carrying it on his person in a concealed fashion (***illegally***) after he became the victim of a robbery, and the perpetrators were two black men (as was Ferguson).

Ferguson relocated to New York where he had lived earlier and again took up residence in the same Flatbush area of NYC where he had previously lived. Apparently, Ferguson had grown unstable mentally. *"Ferguson started taking five showers a day and could be heard by neighbors repeatedly chanting at night, 'all the black people killing all the white people'. [The landlord] became increasingly concerned about Ferguson's obsession with racism and apparent growing mental instability, and asked Ferguson to move out by the end of the month."*[11]

On December 7, 1993, while on a commuter train, Ferguson stood up and began shooting people at random. When all was said and done, six people were dead (including McCarthy's husband) and nineteen had been injured. He had emptied two 15-round magazines.

I realize gun control is an *emotional* issue. Certainly someone in McCarthy's case feels the need to do what she can to limit the purchase of guns with what are termed high-capacity magazines. These hold more than ten rounds. The argument is, why do people need to have a handgun that holds 15 rounds?

---

[11] http://en.wikipedia.org/wiki/Colin_Ferguson_%28convict%29

The better question is, why would someone like Colin Ferguson be able to purchase a gun in the first place? Ultimately, it doesn't matter what laws are enacted, because people like Colin Ferguson, and more recently, Jared Loughner, will always be there. If guns were made illegal for purchase, *they* would still get them.

Obviously, in both Ferguson's and Loughner's cases, neither had a permit to carry a concealed weapon, yet it is just as obvious that both were carrying their weapons in a *concealed* manner. In essence, then, they are both guilty of breaking the law there, even before they shot people.

Had Ferguson or Loughner ever been stopped by police, they would have found the weapon and confiscated it. In most states, carrying a concealed weapon without a permit is a felony. Being found guilty of a felony would have nixed any further chances for either man to purchase another gun through legal channels. Would *that* have stopped them, though? Can anyone say for sure?

So in some ways, while McCarthy and other legislators believe that they need to do what they can to protect the public, it seems that no matter how much they try, the public will never be fully protected.

Within politics, *Liberals* are often seen as attempting to give people *freedom*. The very word "liberal" comes from the Latin meaning "free." So, quite naturally, the politically liberal person would likely believe that women should always have the right to an abortion without question. There should never be any query into *why* a woman is seeking to have an abortion because the woman should always be *free* to obtain an abortion if that is what she chooses to do. No one should stand in the way of a woman's right to *choose* for herself whether she wants to keep her unborn child to full term or to abort it. That is her decision, and liberals believe that they must preserve that option for women at all costs.

At the same time, as we have alluded to, many of these same liberals believe that guns should be outlawed because they are instruments of death. This is the incongruous part for us. Owning a gun is written into the 2nd Amendment. Should it be changed or deleted because some people don't like it that people have guns that can and do kill people?

While guns were created for a number of reasons, which originally included killing for food *and* self-defense, abortion clinics were created for only one purpose: *to kill*. There is no other reason why abortion clinics exist, though proponents of abortion clinics will tell you with a straight face that they also provide education to potential mothers about the baby they are carrying. That is a misnomer because while Planned Parenthood, for instance, has the resources to share with a mother who is considering aborting her unborn child, Planned Parenthood does not make any money from handing out those pamphlets. They make money from their medical procedures, and those medical procedures, more often than not, involve abortion.

It is the same with the area of same-sex unions. Liberals push for what is termed equality for people who want to marry. They argue that we do not stop people of differing cultures from marrying, so how could we work to stop people who share the same genders from marrying? Isn't that promoting *inequality*?

Ultimately, it would appear that liberals who push for women's rights, gay rights, and anti-gun rights have their pet projects just as they would argue that conservatives do. In both cases, there is a sense that Self is being catered to; however, let's take a moment to look at the consequences of some of the positions held by each group.

If liberals believe that women should always have the right to an abortion, conservatives would argue that someone needs to speak up for the *unborn* child. If liberals argue that homosexuals should be given the same rights as heterosexuals where marriage is concerned, conservatives would argue that someone needs to speak up for God and His Word.

If liberals believe that people should not have the right to own a handgun, then we see that while they are fully in favor of a woman having the right to choose 100% of the time without question regarding abortions, they have become contradictory with the issue of guns.

Doesn't it seem odd that the liberals who push for the right of women to destroy the life they carry within them can be so adamantly opposed to a person owning or carrying a gun for the purpose of self-defense in order to *avoid* being killed? On one hand, killing babies is perfectly fine, they say. On the other hand, using a gun to *save* your life or that of your loved ones is *not* acceptable. How does that work? It is because liberals have a very skewed understanding of the value of life. They also have a very unrealistic view of society. They errantly believe that outlawing guns is the same as *eliminating* them. Not true.

Liberals don't seem to mind that millions of babies die through abortion each year (over 1.2 million annually in the U.S. alone). Yet, their hearts bleed *not* for unborn babies, but for criminals who are not treated "fairly" by the system, in spite of what they may have perpetrated against innocent citizens.

In my view, the entire undergirding of liberalism can be seen in its desire to overthrow God's order. That may seem like a very harsh and even dramatic statement to make, but if we consider how often liberals are opposed to God and His Word, it begins to become clear.

Liberals have succeeded in getting prayer tossed out of school. They have been successful in eliminating the use of the Ten Commandments in classrooms. They have pushed to make it legal for women to kill babies. Liberals build big government with lots of taxpayer dollars. In general, liberals believe the larger government is better, but the larger government exists only through greater taxation.

Liberals believe that people who cannot afford things should be given them *free* of charge. Conservatives believe that people should be helped, but should not be helped forever. The government is not there to provide for every need.

My wife's father owns several homes that he routinely rents out. A number of the homes are designated Section 8 housing, which means people with very low income are eligible to rent these homes. With Section 8 housing, the government partially foots the bill, paying rent to the landlord.

Because the government is involved, they have strict guidelines for landlords. My father-in-law just had to have one home inspected before he could rent it out again. The inspector noticed some of the paint on the exterior of the home was peeling. Before the home could pass inspection, the peeling paint needed to be fixed.

The list of things that had to be approved for the home was long. However, what interests me the most is when a person buys a used home today, if some of the paint is peeling, well, it's peeling. No one demands that the peeling paint be repaired. While the potential buyers might request it, the owner is under no compunction to do so.

Yet, when renting a Section 8 home, that home has to be virtually pristine before the government would approve it. The most tragic part is when Section 8 renters *leave*. In nearly all cases, the renters trash the place. In one case, my father-in-law observed that it was obvious that a large man had smashed his body through part of one of the walls. In that same home, toilet seats were broken, sinks cracked, and more. My father-in-law lives right across the street from the homes he owns, which means they did this damage right under his nose.

The same government that ensures that he rents a home that is in extremely good condition had nothing to say about the amount of damage that he was left with when the renters left. This is, of course, part of the problem, because the people living there obviously felt that they were being taken advantage of, so in response to that they left some damage that my father-in-law was left to clean up and repair. This is what happens when people develop that attitude of entitlement. They appreciate nothing and give back the same to society.

If we look at the amount of nonsense that currently exists in society today, it is enough to cause you to want to bury your head. Everyone seems to have an axe to grind with someone or something. Most people are not that happy in life, and because of it they are constantly chasing after the next big deal.

The delusions of Self are many. At every turn, Self cajoles the individual into doing what he/she can to please Self. We are told to live for today. We are told that we should take life by the horns and live life with gusto.

Politics plays a large part in catering to Self. We learn from our leaders and we often find ourselves tricked *by* them as well. Rather than choosing a candidate who seems to be the most qualified for a position, people will often vote for someone because they are more *popular*, or because their peers have opted to vote for that individual, or because news bureaus hype them up more.

Such seemed to be the case with the election of Mr. Obama to this nation's highest office. He came in on a wave of support that seemed like nothing before it. It was extremely uncanny, in my view.

Here was a man who turns out to be little more than a *novelty*. He was the first black man that people really took seriously. Others like Jesse Jackson and Al Sharpton had no chance of success with their previous bids to become president.

Mr. Obama was charismatic while speaking and presented a bit of a hip-looking and -sounding individual that would look good in the Oval Office, yet there were some things missing that the majority did not seem to notice.

During Obama's campaign, the thing we heard repeatedly was that "change is coming." That particular mantra became the chant of the masses. He said little else, and everyone was essentially left on their own to determine what that phrase meant.

This is where Self comes into the picture. For each person, "*change is coming*" likely meant something completely different. Mr. Obama left people to apply their own meaning to his oft-repeated phrase. It didn't matter to him. The media was largely silent about Mr. Obama's past and lack of experience. When people tried to question things about his life, they were ignored or shouted down. It was clear that the media wanted Mr. Obama as the next president, and I would have to say that it is very likely *because* of the media that Mr. Obama *became* president.

The history books would show that Mr. Obama never really explained "change is coming." People would automatically think of President George W. Bush and some of his failures, and they would naturally then conclude that Mr. Obama would do the *opposite*.

Toward the end of Bush's second term, it was clear that the economy was not doing that well at all. However, here we are in 2011, and the economy is doing *far* worse, nearly four years later. This is due to the fact that Mr. Obama has not only *outspent* his predecessor, but has outspent the amount of money that our Federal government takes in each year.

Instead of curtailing spending, Mr. Obama wants the debt ceiling *raised,* and that would mean that he could continue spending money that the government does not have. Had people been able to see what would become of an Obama presidency, they may have thought twice or even three times about voting for him.

The truth is that Self took over, especially among the black community. They wanted a black man in office, and who can blame them? The trouble is that it would have been nice to have a black man in office that actually *cared* about this country. Instead, we seem to have someone in office that cares only about his own goals and aspirations, and whether or not they coincide with the U.S. Constitution doesn't seem to matter.

Politics tends to be a very interesting arena because we have gotten so used to politicians lying to us in one form or another that we simply accept what they say without really even trying to convince ourselves that what they are telling us has major flaws.

This is because of Self. Self doesn't necessarily like the truth when that truth goes against the grain of what Self promotes. These delusions play into the hands of people because it becomes what they seek.

It doesn't matter whether Self is involved in politics, or something else entirely. Self has a way of pushing itself on others and demanding that its desires be met. The more we accommodate Self, the more enslaved we become.

It is tragic when publicly elected officials begin an assault on the U.S. Constitution. Such seems to be the case in Dearborn, MI where both Mayor O'Reilly and Chief of Police Haddad have made their own laws concerning the issue of freedom of speech and expression.

Most of us are familiar with a group that tried to evangelize Muslims at the Arab Festival the past few years. These individuals, though they acted discreetly, were nonetheless harassed and arrested by the police of Dearborn, MI. They were tried, but fortunately acquitted of charges against them.

However, it doesn't stop there, because as I reported previously, Mayor O'Reilly believed he had every right to censure Christians who were simply exercising their right to evangelize through freedom of speech. Of course, he did not actually believe he was censuring anyone. The idea that they were on the sidewalk and not in a pre-approved "booth" with other groups was the issue that the city chose to do battle over. Unfortunately for the city, the 6th District Court of Appeals has overruled the city in a similar case involving a pastor who is an ex-Muslim and was prevented by the Dearborn police department from simply wandering in the festival and discreetly discussing things with individual Muslims.

Dearborn decided that if people are going to exercise freedom of speech, they were going to have to do it their way, which, incidentally, nearly coincided perfectly with Sharia law of Islam.

In the month of April, supporters of Pastor Terry Jones (who burned the Qur'an in protest) gathered in Dearborn, MI. They wanted their voices heard in opposition to radical Muslims who believe that if they become the majority of a certain area, then Islamic law becomes the De Facto law.

During the peaceful gathering of these individuals, Muslims can be seen throwing bottles of liquid on the crowds. The liquid was later determined to be human *urine*. That's nice, isn't it? When Muslims don't get their way, they will stoop to the level of animals in a zoo to get their point across.

And here we were thinking that Islam is a religion of *peace*. The only Muslims who are actually peaceful are those who allegorize the Qur'an and other Islamic writings. Those who take it literally and even literalistically will use any means to get their point across. Assaults, rapes, killings, and now dousing a crowd with human urine are part of the process.

In a recent case, George Saieg sued the city of Dearborn, MI because he believed that his rights had been violated. It turns out that the 6th U.S. Circuit Court of Appeals ruled in his favor, and the ruling is an eye-opener:

"The City may be held liable for the restriction of Saieg's free speech rights that the leafleting restriction caused. A municipality is liable if a constitutional injury results from a policy or custom 'made by its lawmakers or by those whose edicts or acts may fairly be said to represent official policy.' Monell v. Dep't of Soc. Servs., 436 U.S. 658, 694–95 (1978). In this case, the City approved the Festival 'subject to . . . the rules and regulations of the Police Department.' R. 47-13 (Ex. M: Council Resolution)...Chief Haddad described the leafleting policy as his department's policy, subject only to the approval of the city council and the mayor. R. 47-11 (Ex. K: Haddad Dep. at 95–96) (stating that 'the police department will supply the standards that must be met,' such as the 'prohibition of individuals handing out . . . materials on the public sidewalk'). The police department's leafleting policy, made with the authority that the City Council delegated to it, fairly represents official City policy. **Therefore, Saieg may hold the City liable for violating his First Amendment right to free speech**"[12] (emphasis in original).

What the court found to be patently clear is that the city of Dearborn, MI, was guilty of placating Muslims by adopting rules that were *favourable* to Sharia law. This is unconscionable because it completely

---

[12] http://www.andrewbostom.org/blog/2011/05/29/first-amendment-trumps-sharia-in-dearborn/

overrides the U.S. Constitution of the United States, where people are guaranteed the right to express themselves freely. Certainly, there are laws that prohibit certain actions during the commission or expression of freedom of speech, and in the case of Saieg, he simply wanted the freedom to indiscriminately wander the festival and strike up conversation with Arabs discreetly. The city wanted him in a booth, and they wanted him to stay in that booth.

The problem, of course, is that a Muslim will not come up to a booth that is clearly labeled a "Christian" booth (having the word "Bible" in it, etc.). If they know that the people in that booth are Christians, they will also know that they are there for the purpose of *proselytizing*. No Muslim – who wants to avoid being harassed or executed by his own – will deliberately go up to a booth to get into conversations with Christians.

However, a Christian walking through the festival will not draw attention to himself, and in Saieg's case, he *was* a Muslim and therefore understands what Muslims believe and how they think. In other words, he is in a better position than most Christians to evangelize Muslims. The city wanted to curtail his efforts. The court overturned that, siding with Saieg.

The tragedy of Dearborn, MI is that they are willingly and seemingly with malice setting aside the U.S. Constitution in favor of Sharia law, whether they think so or not. The court has obviously stated that this is exactly what they are doing and it needs to stop.

We have Mayor O'Reilly and Chief of police Haddad to thank for setting aside the U.S. Constitution, in favor of Sharia. What I'm hearing or reading about in many places throughout Europe and now in the United States is that Muslims firmly believe that they can impose Sharia law on the populace of their newly "adopted" country. They do this through force and through the political system. This is

Self at its worst. By attempting to force specific views on a populace by whatever means necessary, Self has taken over the assault.

Islam removes certain freedoms that are guaranteed under the Constitution. Because radical Muslims believe they have a mandate from Allah, they also believe that any means at their disposal to affect change is fair game. In reality, this is nothing more than Self gaining the upper hand. While as a Christian, I object to issues such as abortion on demand, same-sex unions, and the like, I do not believe that I have the authority to overthrow the existing societal values in favor of Christianity. I am a stranger here, with my citizenship being in heaven. Certainly, I can and should do what is necessary within the confines of the law to affect change, I am prohibited from using violent measures to achieve such results.

Many radical Muslims believe that they can pretend to be friendly to non-Muslims, even lying to their face, the plain fact of the matter is that for the authentic Christian, no such duplicitous demeanor is to be used. We are to do what we can and leave things in the Lord's hands. This is the opposite of Self, because we are making way for the Lord to do what He will do and recognizing that His purposes are far superior to ours. Islam thinks nothing of killing those who stand in their way. This is Self attempting vainly to show its alleged superiority over everyone else.

Interestingly enough, the city of Dearborn is still playing favorites toward Muslims. This past June, 2011 (nearly one month *after* George Saig and his case in court), protestors appeared at the Arab Festival with signs and placards stating that Islam is a religion of blood and murder. Of course, Arabs/Muslims were not pleased, yet as Pamela Geller states, "*Indeed. But bus ads and billboards that myriad Muslim groups ran claiming that Abraham, Issac, Jacob and*

Moses were Muslims were deeply offensive and 'dirty' to non-Muslims. Nobody was attacked."[13]

Robert Spencer of *Jihad Watch* indicated that the ads Geller referred to were on city buses, yet in spite of a court *win*, Spencer's ads were *not* allowed to run. Things seemed to begin way back on June 26, 2009. "*In Dearborn, Michigan, where the local mosque's call to prayer is broadcast over the town by loudspeakers, a group of Christian evangelists were told that they could not pass out Bibles on the sidewalk during a festival. This is part of a growing national trend to disfavor Christian expression and traditional speech, and reflects a disturbing direction in public policy in America today.*"[14]

The mayor and police chief of Dearborn both *say* they support the U.S. Constitution, but then offer their own opinion that public safety somehow *trumps* free speech that is guaranteed by the Constitution. Obviously, it cannot be both ways. Either you support the U.S. Constitution and the people's right to free speech and peaceful assembly, or you do not. To hide behind the "we're concerned about public safety" line is just that, a *line*.

What the mayor winds up doing is simply placating Muslims and discriminating against Christians. In fact, it is very clear from past situations that Muslims are the ones who became violent, not Christians. So under the guise of "public safety," the mayor prefers to quash Christians' rights and winds up siding with Muslims, whether he thinks so or not. Certainly the Muslims in this case know exactly what is going on.

It is clear that Dearborn has become noted for its pro-Muslim position, whether they see it that way or not. "*Dearborn is one of the most densely populated Muslim communities in the United States. It*

---

[13] http://www.jihadwatch.org/2011/06/dearborn-michigan-muslims-physically-attack-christian-groups.html (06/25/2011)
[14] http://spectator.org/archives/2009/06/26/a-religious-test (06/25/2011)

has the largest Mosque in North America. In the past few years Dearborn has gained national attention for taking a pro-Muslim stance and for the arrest and intimidation of Christian evangelists for engaging in protected speech activity."[15]

So where is the equality for Christians? It seems to be going the way of the dinosaur. *"Four years ago, a federal judge in Indiana who has been nominated by President Barack Obama to the Seventh Circuit appeals court, David Hamilton, ordered that prayers in the Indiana statehouse could be offered to 'Allah' but could not be offered in the name of 'Jesus.' (This suit was later dismissed by the Seventh Circuit, on which Judge Hamilton will now sit.)"*[16]

The reality, though, is that these Muslims who have come to this country from elsewhere have done so *voluntarily*. They *chose* to come here. It is clear that radical Muslims are here to change it from within. Out with the Constitution and in with Sharia! They gather together in areas of this country where politicians and leaders are favorable to them and will willingly adopt Islamic customs. Before these politicians and leaders realize it, they are bending the laws toward Sharia. Once again, this is the height of selfishness. Can you imagine moving to and living in a new country and expecting that country to change to suit *you*? This is the core of Islamic teaching and it is nothing but Self in religious garb.

In the beginning, the individuals who were sensitive to the beliefs and practices of Muslims believed they were simply being respectful of another culture – in this case, Islam. Eventually, they bent over backwards to placate a group that they know will become violent if they do not cave into their demands. This is happening wherever Muslims take over an area through large population growth.

---

[15] http://www.boogai.net/constitution/christian-pastor%E2%80%99s-free-speech-victory-against-city-of-dearborn/ (06/25/2011)

[16] http://spectator.org/archives/2009/06/26/a-religious-test (06/25/2011)

Instead of coming to this country and adopting the ways of America, they are here to overthrow those ways. If they cannot win through the political arena, they will use force. They believe they are allowed to protest and block traffic and demand their way, but when Americans gather to peacefully support the right of Terry Jones (or anyone else) to burn a Qur'an, they have to step in and stop the process or at least throw urine on it.

This is the mentality of radical Muslims. Yet I see bumper stickers that use religious symbols to spell out "Co-exist." Sorry, it is clear that radical Muslims are not interested in co-existence. They are only interested in overcoming by opposing anything that they believe stands against Sharia law. Authentic Christians cannot co-exist in the sense that the world means it, either. We can live peacefully among the world, but we cannot join in with the world's godless attitude.

I will stand opposed to radical Islam because of all the inequities, pain, and violence that are associated with it. Muslims who are peaceful automatically have my respect. Those who believe that they have the right to lord it over others or bombard others with their own radical viewpoints on pain of violence or death should not be tolerated.

There is no use for this type of thinking in a civilized society. It exists and will only grow in an environment that allows it to do so. Dearborn, MI has become one of those places, but fortunately for the U.S. Constitution, courts are becoming a wall against the encroachment of Islam and Sharia law, a system that does not respect the value of human life.

Why do politicians seemingly give in to pressure groups like Islam? In this case, why did Mayor O'Reilly side with Islamists against people who were exercising their right of free speech? It seems simple enough, and it almost always boils down to this reason: *Self.* I believe once a person is elected to public office and finds that he/she likes it, the goal then becomes to *remain* in public office.

Let's face it. With public service, whether as a member of a city council, a mayor, a senator, or president, people who are involved in politics in that type of capacity can quickly become enamored with the job. It becomes a game to determine how to "spin" things so that the voting public believes that you should remain in your job during the next election cycle.

In the case of Mayor O'Reilly, I can see him buckling to the pressure foisted upon him by the ever-burgeoning number of Muslims in the Dearborn, MI area. Since they are increasingly becoming a larger portion of the electorate, so to speak, it behooves any publicly elected official to not only *note* their presence, but to do what he/she can to *gain* their support, even if that means taking their side against the U.S. Constitution.

In essence, Mayor O'Reilly is doing what any pragmatic public official would do. He wants to court those within his city so that when it comes time for re-election, he will be in a favorable position to win, remaining in office for another term.

This is the problem, though, with politics as a whole. Once a person begins to benefit from their job as a publicly-elected official, they will often at the very least be tempted to compromise their own belief system in order to *remain* in office. Self is at the root of this, and that much is clear.

I imagine it becomes a very difficult road to travel because on one hand, a person elected to public office has their own set of beliefs, yet they must now represent – for the most part – the people who elected them. If they do a good job, they will likely become re-elected. If not, they will be voted out, replaced with someone who the public believes will do a better job.

As a "for instance," in today's day and age, it is virtually impossible to get elected if the person running does not support a woman's right to choose to abort any and all her unborn children. If a person – especially a man – stands up and announces that he morally opposes abortion, the chances of that person being elected are greatly reduced to just about nothing. This is the case, unless he/she happens to be in a district that overwhelmingly opposes abortion on demand.

So consider the person who runs for office yet is morally opposed to abortion on demand. In order to run and become elected, he/she would virtually have to say that they would support a woman's right to choose, even if they did not. So let's say they become elected. Right from the start, they hold a position on an extremely important hot-button issue that is different from the majority of people who elected them, but has promised to support it.

Would they spend their time in office compromising their beliefs every time the issue of abortion came up? They would have to, or if they voted with their conscience, they would likely not be re-elected.

The area of politics is an area that demands people make hard choices, and most of those hard choices have to do with whether or not a particular position is adopted based on a person's moral compass or based on the wants of those who elected that person to office in the first place. From Mayor O'Reilly's perspective, I'm sure he simply did not want trouble during the Muslim Festival, so he opted to make the public sidewalk off-limits to people who wanted to proselytize.

While it may have seemed like a good idea at the time, the truth is – as the court noted – that Mayor O'Reilly and the police department severely overstepped their bounds by removing rights that are guaranteed under Federal documents of this country.

I firmly believe that it is nearly impossible for anyone who seeks public office to enter into that office without compromising their own particular value system. For many mayors today, they are certainly aware that groups like Gays and Lesbians want to have parades through their city on Gay Pride day (or week, or month). The mayor then, in most cases, may be expected to not only give permission for the event, but support it. Sometimes, that support is expected to include actually being part of that parade.

So, imagine a Christian mayor of some city that holds a Gay Pride parade, and it is the expected role of the mayor to be the Grand Marshall of said parade. What does one do? For the life of me, I cannot picture Jesus being the Grand Marshall of such a parade. At the same time, I cannot picture Jesus being the Grand Marshall of nearly *any* parade.

In order to be a successful politician, it takes a willingness to scratch some other politician's back while they scratch yours. The entire process of politicizing takes on an overtone of compromise from the start. In the back of a person's mind is the constant picture of the people who elected you to office. What about them? How do you support them while making your own decisions?

More and more today, people like mayors do not simply make decisions based on morals. However, the moral question comes into the situation often and must be addressed, not ignored. Self has its way of addressing issues, and rarely is Self's way the best way.

Chapter 13

Self in Islam

Interestingly enough, what I see happening in today's world is something that causes people to become far more *segregated* than in the past. Today, there seems to be *greater* distrust among the races and ethnicities. Mr. Obama stated that his would be a transparent administration and he would work to bring the races together (my paraphrase), yet he has not done that. In fact, the opposite seems to have occurred because of the discriminatory policies of people like Attorney General Eric Holder.

I believe with the full frontal assault of women's groups, Gay and Lesbian groups, and even Islam, our global society is becoming far more fractured than ever. Islam is presented to the world as a peaceful religion. It tries to endear itself to everyone by claiming that it is the true path to love and peace. The problem, of course, is that juxtaposed against these thoughts are the real-life crimes of militant Muslims who want nothing more than to kill all non-Muslims, especially if those non-Muslims are Jewish.

This belief, followed by action, is tragic. Because there are Muslims who think like this, they have no compunction against committing some of the most brutal crimes ever noted. They believe that they are on Allah's side.

Not long ago, in Thailand, several murders took place, and the perpetrators were radical Muslims who believe that Buddhism is not only an affront to Islam and therefore Allah, but something that should be eradicated. As usual, the radical Muslims make their point *gruesomely*. This is taking place in a country where Muslims are a *small* minority, yet they obviously know how to make their presence felt through inexplicable and ferocious violence. Need I say that this is nothing more than Self? This is what Islam creates, a strong desire to serve Self. Killing people wantonly, becoming a martyr for Islam – all of it stems from the desires of Self. When a suicide bomber blows himself up, he firmly believes that he will gain 70 virgins in the next life. The Christian, on the other hand, will spend eternity *serving* the Lord perfectly. Which version showcases Self?

In one such case, a 9-year-old boy was killed. The body of this boy was lying not far from another child of much younger age. Both had been gruesomely beheaded. How can this happen? Is this merely an anomaly or exception to the rule? It does not appear to be the case.

The information provided in an article regarding the situation is easily verifiable from a number of sources. *"More than 4,000 people from police and teachers to monks and children have been killed in the past 7 years by Muslims in southern Thailand, but hardly a word in the mainstream media. In Southern Thailand Muslim gunmen continue killing and threatening innocent citizens. The Muslim insurgents have threatened to kill 20 teachers and have distributed fliers that said, 'WANTED: 20 Deaths of Buddhist teachers.' Muslim terrorists object to the education system which teaches Buddhist culture that is not acceptable in Islam. The attacks are intended to force Buddhists to leave the region because Muslims want to create an independent Muslim nation in the three southern provinces."*[17]

Please be warned that if you choose to follow the link in the footnote on the bottom of this page, you will witness a video of the situation *after* the murders took place, which shows the bodies of the two young boys. Do *not* go there unless you have a strong stomach.

Folks, this is nothing less than *satanic*. What we are witnessing throughout the world is the rise of a death cult that will stop at nothing to achieve its agenda. The radical Muslim believes he is on the correct path and the world stands against him. He reacts to the world first by calling us "infidels," and then after labeling us in this way, feels justified in killing us. Truly, Islam is at war with the world, not the other way around.

While there are certainly moderate Muslims in this world, Muslims who outwardly mean no harm to anyone, it is impossible for a Muslim to be a "good" Islamist. Being so means that they undertake the same methods and walk the same path that Muhammad walked. He lived by the sword, wantonly killing any and all who opposed him.

The ideology of Islam distinguishes between two groups: Muslims and infidels. If you are not one of the former, you are of the latter designation, and you will eventually be given the opportunity to convert or die.

In the case of the terror that radical Muslims visit upon innocent people throughout the world, many times people are not given the

---

[17] http://barenakedislam.wordpress.com/2011/05/09/thailand-muslims-behead-a-9-year-old-boy-warning-graphic-images/ (06/24/2011)

opportunity to address their situation. They are simply and brutally killed.

We hear today from leading Imams that Islam is a "religion of peace," and that anyone who does not convert to Islam will be treated with respect and provided the basic needs to live. Why is it then that we see so much Muslim-on-non-Muslim violence? Is this their definition of receiving the basics of life? Is this what they mean by being treated with respect? Moreover, is this their understanding and teaching of Islam as a peaceful religion? No, what they are teaching is nothing more than dhimmitude. This is *slavery* under Islamic rule.

Those who do not convert to Islam and are *not* killed will probably wish they were put out of their misery. It is clear the world over that radical Muslims rape women and girls, kill those with whom they disagree, and commit other atrocities that the world is supposed to ignore. Certainly, the liberal media ignores most of that, because if people were given the opportunity to see the real Islam, it would horrify and incense most. The liberal media has its own agenda.

Islam is an *ideology* passing itself off as a religion. It purports to be superior to all other ideologies and religions. I don't mind that they boast of that. I don't mind that they claim to be the only true religion. That's not what bothers me, because as an authentic Christian, I do the same thing. There is, of course, one huge difference. I do not – as radical Muslims do – run around killing those who refuse to accept my understanding of Christianity. I do not protest and demand the removal of freedom of speech if someone says something offensive to me or about Jesus or the Bible. I do not strap bombs to my body nor do I encourage others to do that.

What I do is *educate*. I try to point out what I believe are the fallacies of other religious systems, ideologies, and dogmas. Of course, while that may appear to be self-aggrandizing and even egotistical, stop to consider the fact that all people who believe they are correct about something do this same thing. Jesus Himself said that He is the way, the truth, and the life and that no one would come to the Father except through Him (cf. John 14:6). I'm simply repeating His teachings as I understand them.

When I see a billboard or ad somewhere presented by Muslims stating that Allah is the same as the God of the Bible, I am repelled. When I see or hear these folks attempting to make connections between Allah and Abraham, Issac, Jacob, and even Jesus, it angers me because I fully believe Allah is Satan in disguise. There is *nothing* within the Qur'an that is in line with Christianity. Every false religion – of which I believe Islam to be one – began by the efforts of one entity – *Satan*. Because of this, there is no connection at all between Islam and Christianity.

Not long ago, in response to one of my blogs, a writer told me that while he was troubled by actions of radical Muslims, he wished they would see that we all have the same God. I tried to be as polite as possible and told him that we do not have the same God. The god of Islam and the God of the Bible have nothing in common. I cannot lie about that to make the writer feel good. To do so is a tremendous disservice to him. He needs to know the truth.

This is what I do not understand about some churches today that are entering into relationships with Islam. They embrace Islam as if there *is* a connection between Christianity and Islam! This past February, Rick Warren seemed to lead the way down such a path. In a speech to Muslims, Rick Warren stated, "*Before we 'shake your hand' in responding to your letter, we ask forgiveness of the All-Merciful One and of the Muslim community around the world.*"[18]

Chrislam – the embracing of Islam within Christian churches – is on the rise in America. On June 26, 2011 (tomorrow, as I write this),

---

[18] http://www.nowtheendbegins.com/blog/?p=1366

many Christian churches across America will officially embrace Chrislam. As noted, this movement was begun by Rick Warren of Saddleback Church. I guess Mr. Warren sees no compromise in what he's doing. It shouldn't surprise us, because if we follow Warren's history, we learn that he has a deep connection with Robert Schuller. That is pretty much common knowledge today.

Roughly 70 churches and one seminary (in New York State) across the United States are scheduled to participate in the event. It can be as simple as having a Rabbi, a Pastor, and an Imam taking turns reading from their sacred texts. Certainly to have a Jewish Rabbi reading from the Old Testament is fine, but to have an Imam reading from the Qur'an? Come on, Rick. Did God inspire that as well? For the churches participating in this event, they would have to argue that the Qur'an is just as important as the Bible. Obviously, for this to truly be a Chrislam event, Muslims must participate.

But what are these churches saying to these Muslims (or Jews)? They are saying that salvation is not important and that it is not specific to Christianity. Folks, this is the Emergent Church at its worst, downplaying authentic salvation by embracing everyone's ideals. Does anyone honestly believe that radical Muslims will take this route? If so, will they do so *sincerely*?

If someone rejects Jesus' teachings, I do not chase after them and slit their throats or behead them. Jesus did not do that, and in fact, He never even chased *after* anyone.

So while it is fine to believe that my beliefs are the correct ones, it would only become egotistical if I somehow tried to enforce that belief with *force*. There were any number of people who did that from the 3rd century onward within Roman Catholicism and it was wrong. It is still wrong today, yet we have ample examples of the fact that it continues to occur.

The saddest part of all this, aside from the fact that people are dying through brutal acts of horror by radical Muslims, as described in this chapter, is that the world will likely not waken to it until it is way too late. We know from the many references in the book of Revelation that the Antichrist will lead a war against all who refuse to worship him or his image. He will be the most brutal dictator to ever rise.

What we are seeing now throughout the world is the *preparation* that is building up to that time. But, of course, God is not silent. He still continues to call those who hear His voice from the kingdom of darkness to His Kingdom of Light. Salvation is the only thing that will ultimately save people from the coming world holocaust. It is individual and it is a personal choice.

The two young boys who are shown dead in the video may not have ever had a chance to receive Jesus as Savior/Lord. If you are reading this, then know that you *do* have a chance. I hope you will take the time to ask Him to reveal to you His truth, and once seen, you will embrace it. For more information, you can turn to the last chapter of this book.

Chapter 14
Self in Legalism

I am 54 years old. That's how many years I've been alive, and only God knows how many more years He has given me before He takes me home. I was thinking today about some of the churches I have attended throughout my life. The first one I recall was when I was about five, and it happened to be a Presbyterian Church in the small town in New York State where I spent part of my life.

Being that age, what can you appreciate (or not) about what is taught? I remember hearing about the baby Jesus during Christmas time, but other than that, not much. I'm sure that was not the fault of the minister. I was five, or younger.

I also recall spending time as a member of a Baptist Church in the same state. This was way into my teen years and into junior college days. The preaching was good, and because of my attendance at that church I wound up attending Philadelphia College of Bible, from which I graduated with a Bachelor's in Bible degree.

After graduating from Philadelphia Bible College, I went back to my town where I attended the Baptist Church. However, I wanted to be in ministry, so I kept my eyes and ears open for positions in the area. I found one at another Baptist Church in my area. At that point, due to my limited experience in a variety of churches, I thought one Baptist Church was like all the rest. I soon learned that a GARBC (General Association of Regular Baptist Churches) was far different from the Independent Baptist Church, or the ABC (American Baptist Churches). All of them had their particular slant on the biblical doctrines.

This particular church I was at was quite liberal and, in many ways, humanistic. There seemed to be little emphasis on God's work in the world and more emphasis on the work of people in the world. Through discussion with the pastor, he encouraged me to go to seminary or graduate school. I applied and was accepted at Eastern Baptist Theological Seminary in Philadelphia. I went there and my entire world shattered. Had I known about this type of liberalism that was prevalent at Eastern, I never would have gone.

Don't get me wrong. I do think that the first step in growing is often found in asking questions. Questions are important and they should be asked. However, after one semester there, I began to doubt everything. If someone asked me to prove that the Bible had veracity, it would have been difficult.

I recall one professor who essentially turned Jesus' miracles into natural events. For instance, when He calmed the sea, He simply stood up when He "guessed" the squall would end and told it to be quiet. Classmates seemed fine with that. For me, I thought "How asinine is that to believe?" Jesus was not a fisherman. If anyone know about the windstorms and squalls on the Sea of Galilee, it would have been Peter and the other fisherman with Jesus. Since they had far more experience on the sea, would they not have known that the squall was going to end soon? If so, would Jesus have been able to fool them, as my professor implied? Of course, let's not forget that if Jesus had really done that, He would have been guilty of something that qualified as sin.

I left seminary disillusioned and without graduating. From that point onward, I attended churches that were more liberal in their beliefs from what I had been used to, and as I consider it, I spent many years being thoroughly dissatisfied with my faith. Not much made sense, and God did not even seem that important.

Such is the result of attending liberal institutions and churches. They tend to peel away your beliefs, and if you are not well-grounded in the faith, you will lose quite a bit. Liberal churches and institutions tend to be one extreme within Christendom.

It was really many years after these experiences that God seemed to simply wake me up one day. I was attending a Presbyterian Church in the area with my wife and I noticed that the preaching had become so boring, I had actually gotten into the habit of bringing my own book to read! I couldn't figure out what had happened. Of course, I found out later that Emergent theology had moved in, based largely on Rick Warren's view of things.

As I sat there one Sunday morning – hating it and wishing above all things that I could be anywhere else – a thought hit me out of the blue. The thought was that I should go to seminary and obtain my master's degree. That was weird. I scribbled a note to my wife, who read it and smiled.

When I got home that day, I began looking on the Internet for graduate schools and found one that would allow me to do things via the Internet and at home. I was impressed with their curriculum, so I applied, was accepted and began my studies. I loved it! I was learning, and I felt as though I was on a firm foundation.

I also looked for and found a different church. This new one was far more fundamental in its beliefs. We began attending and wound up joining. Eventually, I completed my studies and received my Master's in Biblical Studies degree from Tyndale Theological Seminary in Texas.

A year or so ago, we left that church after being there for roughly four years. I had become a regular teacher of Adult Bible classes at the church, as well as a deacon. There were a few things I did not realize then, though, that I fully realize now. Had I known these things then, I would not have stayed at the church.

You see, liberal churches are very easy to spot, as far as I'm concerned. They water down the gospel. They fabricate areas surrounding Jesus while de-emphasizing important aspects of His Person. These things are obvious to anyone who knows anything about the Bible because what is taught at liberal places simply does not gel with Scripture. That becomes easy to see.

The church we attended for roughly four years was right on, biblically speaking. In other words, I believed (and still do) that their doctrinal statement and beliefs are biblically correct. What I've learned is that this is only part of the picture that should be considered when trying to find a church or institution to attend.

What I realize now about that church is that it is fundamentalism gone awry. While they emphasize the correct beliefs (in my view), they do so to the point that many individuals have become legalistic.

This is the other extreme within Christendom, and at times it is far more difficult to see.

Let me explain. While on one hand, you have a group of people who gather on Sundays and Wednesdays and for other social events in the church, you also have people who can be rather hard on one another.

In a liberal setting, people tend to be very forgiving and accepting of others. There is a happiness (I won't say "joy") here that is sometimes absent from other places. I was reading A. W. Tozer recently and he essentially said the same thing. Many of the churches that are fundamentally correct are often dead spiritually. Because they often focus on the letter of the law, people become really touchy about certain subjects. Emphasis is always on the external for some reason.

This fact escapes many within these types of churches. They often hide behind Scripture and use it as a hammer to beat people over the head with when they feel it is needed. After all, it's in the Bible, therefore we must follow it. I would agree; however, it needs to be followed with the correct attitude.

I guess for me the difference is found in two different types of people in the Bible. On one hand, you have the rich young ruler who believed that he had "arrived" because of all the wonderful things he did for others throughout his life. In essence, he really came to Jesus so that Jesus would simply pronounce him "clean" and "justified." He went away very sad because he unfortunately worshiped his riches too much to be willing to give them away and follow Jesus. This man needed Jesus as we all do, but he walked away from Him.

On the other hand, we have the religious leaders of Jesus' day who brought before Him the woman caught in the very act of adultery. I've always wondered how they found this woman. Were they peeping through her window or tent – all in the name of obedience to the law, of course – or did they accidentally discover what was going on behind closed doors? The reality is that however they discovered her, they thought she should be stoned to death and brought her to Jesus to find out if He would uphold the law or ignore it.

I also note that they did not bring the man with them. They only brought the *woman*, and unless she was part of Sex Without Partners, she was obviously involved in an adulterous situation with someone. If she was a prostitute, then there was still a man involved, but apparently the religious leaders did not feel the need to prosecute him or demand his death.

We know how the story goes. Jesus began writing in the dirt, but we do not know what He wrote. When the religious leaders kept insisting that He become judge and jury of the situation, He simply said that the person without sin should cast the first stone. Of course, when the truth of that statement sunk in, no one could throw anything, not even their own puffed-up feelings of self-importance.

That's the interesting thing about legalists. They are often out for blood – someone else's blood. They are unable to see their own faults and foibles unless someone points them out, and when they do, they attack. They have no love for their neighbor. Their only desire is to be better than their neighbor and to make sure that their neighbor knows it. If the neighbor is not aware of it, they'll be happy to inform them – repeatedly, if necessary.

Legalists have little to no grace to offer anyone. While they may go through the motions, there is nothing real there inside them. Liberals have more than enough grace – too much – to offer people.

I recall teaching at the church I've referred to. I realize I don't know everything about the Bible. I have a long way to go before that happens, and in fact, it won't happen in this life. Nonetheless, it was always interesting to me to experience situations in which some individuals (always the same ones) would try to test my mettle. They questioned what I said and why I said it, and even though they likely knew what I meant, they needed to hear it said in words they were used to using. After all, I could have been hiding my own meaning in words that they were not used to hearing, you know, like people from cults do routinely. If they disagreed with me over how I explained a particular doctrine, they let me know about it.

I recall one situation in which I tried to explain what Paul meant by being truly Jewish and what made someone a "spiritual" Jew from Romans 9-11. Several people in the group assured me they were spiritual Jews though they were Gentile. I tried to explain that Paul was referring only to actual Jews who were also true believers, not Jews in culture or ethnicity only. This made them spiritual Jews. The context was in the fact that Paul was talking about Jews, not Gentiles. But these individuals had come along and pulled verses out of context to show that they – Gentiles – were actually spiritually Jewish. No, if anything, they were believing Gentiles. Becoming a Christian did not somehow make them Jewish, either physically or spiritually. Some folks took offense to my comments and did not return to my class.

On another occasion, we were discussing some of the things Jesus did in His post-resurrection body – you know, like walking through walls and disappearing immediately, yet being able to eat food. He wasn't a ghost, yet His resurrection body was far different from the one He had prior to His death. I pointed out that this type of body may also be the type of body that we – as believers in the next life – will enjoy. Well, you would think I had tried to tell people that they were actually gods!

I'm convinced (though I certainly could be wrong) that our glorified bodies will be able to do far more than our current bodies can do now. I fully expect to never get sick, never overeat, never have to fight the battle of the bulge, never have to get laser eye surgery, never have to go to the dentist and more. I also believe that I will be able to walk through walls because I believe that in our current state we are only able to live within our four dimensions (length, width, depth, and time), but after this life, when the Lord gives me a glorified body, many more dimensions will open up to me, and what would appear as walking through walls now will merely be going from one dimension to another.

There were many occasions in which the same few individuals would question what I was teaching because it did not gel with their understanding of what the Bible taught. They weren't really interested in my explanation. They simply wanted to trap me or prove that I was not correct. When you have people in your class who come with their own notes, ask a question based on those notes, but swear to you that they don't know one way or another, something is wrong. This is legalism because my explanation and understanding of Scripture did not fit into their exceedingly narrow understanding of things biblical.

I recall years ago when I was between the ages of 16 – 18, and I had mentioned to a co-worker (who was a fundamentalist) my interest in the Charismatic movement. Of course, that was before I had really taken the time to study the subject to see what the Bible said. I also had not seen the excesses that the Charismatic movement became known for (and is still known for today). I simply mentioned it, and his response was pure anger! That took me by surprise, to say the least. All of a sudden he became the dad and I was the son and he was going to let me know in no uncertain terms of my error.

He reminds me of one of the religious leaders who found the woman committing adultery and so thought he had her future mapped out. Fortunately, God did not respond that way at all, and because He did not, He gained another follower.

Two extremes: *liberalism* and *legalism*. Both are wrong and both are really cut from the same cloth; the desire to elevate and please *Self*. They both stem from people who believe that they know better than God does.

I recall too many unfortunate situations occurring in that fundamental church I attended. People were at each other's throats and they would say things that would sting or wound, yet at the same time, those people who often left the largest wounds cried the loudest when someone did something to hurt them, whether it was real or perceived.

Neither liberalism nor legalism has its place in God's house, in my opinion. Both are extremes brought about by a complete lack of understanding where God and His Word is concerned, along with the strong desire for Self to become and remain supreme. I want to be clear here. I'm not talking about believing the *fundamentals of the faith*. I'm talking about believing the fundamentals of the faith to a point that everything narrows into a very legalistic view of life. It's just as wrong as the liberal who believes that God loves, therefore all paths lead to Him, one way or another. Both viewpoints completely miss the boat in my opinion. Both viewpoints are born of Self, because both views aim to please Self above all things. Whatever *seems* right, *is* right, regardless of what God's Word teaches. Self then becomes the deciding factor.

I'm far more discerning about what church I will attend these days. I look for a tight ship doctrinally speaking, but I also look for a church that is liberal with love. I believe we have found such a church, and the difference is remarkably stark. I can and will do without both extremes because God seems to be in neither.

There is a way to understand the fundamental doctrines of the faith, while at the same time be bursting with love and compassion for our fellow human beings, and especially for those within the household of faith. This needs to exist and it too often does not.

By God's grace, I will not make that mistake again.

Chapter 15
Self and Truth

It's been a long time in coming, but the lawmakers and courts in The Netherlands have finally made it official: Geert Wilders has been found not guilty of hate crimes! We can rejoice that radical Islam has been foiled, at least a bit. Will they give up? Of course not. In fact, it is very likely that Wilders will continue to face death threats.

Wilders' "crime" was that he had the audacity to make true statements about Islam. Muslims did not like that and countered that he was making "hateful" statements, which in turn, under The Netherlands' law, should be treated as a hate crime. Even though the prosecution originally obliged, they eventually argued in court that Wilders should be acquitted.

The idea that someone can make a truthful statement about Islam, Muhammad, or a facet of another religion and be labeled a "hater" is ridiculous, but it is happening. It is the newest politically correct method of silencing your critics.

For instance, prior to Mr. Obama's election, it was common to hear comments like, "This country will never elect a black man to be president!" It was a "triple dog dare ya" with racial overtones.

Now that he's been elected and has done nothing but move this country toward the brink of financial disaster, the comment of any person (who is not black or another minority) who deigns to criticize Mr. Obama brings an immediate cry of "racism." I've heard the liberal media making that claim too many times. The truth is that Mr. Obama has taken what George W. Bush left us with and made it far worse.

Prior to becoming elected, Mr. Obama pointedly asked the question, "You need to ask yourself, are you better off today than you were four years ago?" This, of course, pointed back to Bush's tenure as president.

Of course, the exact same question can and should be asked of our current president. The response to it would be cries of racism or the complaint that Mr. Obama needs four more years. To do what, finish destroying what is left of America?!

When it becomes impossible to fight the facts, it's always far easier and more politically correct to play the race card. We're seeing it with respect to Mr. Obama, and we are seeing it where Islam is concerned.

Over the past week, I've spent some time reading about the constant demands of Muslims throughout our world. Moreover, I've learned how they treat those who are not Muslims, as in the case of Egypt and Tunisia.

First, I read a brief report today stating that due to "modesty" claims, Muslim nurses have been given permission by the United Kingdom to not have to wash their hands. In essence, because radical Muslim women argue that showing their hands in public is an affront to Allah, they must refrain from doing so, and since it is impossible to wash your hands without exposing them, they need to be given a pass. So what does the U.K. do? Gives them a pass.

Just this week, two Muslim men who converted to Islam were arrested *"for plotting to blow up a military recruitment center in Seattle. The facility also houses a day care center."*[19]

The article goes onto say, *"The two men were identified as Abu Khalid Abdul-Latif (formerly known as Joseph Anthony Davis) and Walli Mujahidh (formerly known as Frederick Domingue, Jr.). Abdul-Latif and Mujahidh tried to recruit a third man but he went to the authorities instead. It is worth noting that the third man (who has not been identified) met Abdul-Latif and Mujahidh while serving in prison. Naturally, one wonders if they converted to Islam during their incarceration."*[20]

Speaking of prison conversions to Islam, this is another reason why we need people like Rep. Peter King, who is holding hearings on just this problem, in spite of what Rep. Sheila Jackson Lee and others are complaining about.

---

[19] http://spectator.org/blog/2011/06/23/two-muslim-converts-arrested-f?utm_source=UndergroundBunker&utm_medium=twitter#
[20] Ibid

There are videos on the 'Net that show mobs of riot-ready Muslims, seemingly intent on burning down a synagogue in Tunisia. In Egypt, mobs of rioting Muslims deliberately set fire to churches, killing twelve people and injuring 200.

In Dearborn, MI, at the recent Arab Festival, videographers were assaulted with spit, and video shows a number of "loving" Muslims flipping off the camera. Even though a "Peacekeeping Team" was present, nothing was done and no one that I know of was arrested. You have to hand it to Mayor O'Reilly, who has obviously learned that catering to Islam means job security, or so he hopes.

I was driving my wife to work recently and we discussed these things. I admitted to her that it would be extremely difficult to roll over and play dead if I or my family met this type of radicalized activity from Muslims. For instance, if I saw an entire group of Muslims blocking the street to pray toward Mecca, I would be very tempted to walk right through them.

Of course, I would be accused of not respecting them; however, it would be clear that if that event took place, Muslims are the ones who are not respecting our laws here in the United States.

I am certainly not saying that Muslims should not be free to practice their religion. The problem begins when Muslims believe they are not required to obey our laws, or if they push hard enough, they will receive special dispensations not given to anyone else. This is absurd and is completely contrary to our U.S. Constitution.

People should be allowed to burn the Qur'an without fear of reprisals. People burn the U.S. flag. They burn Bibles. I don't get in their faces about it. It's one way that people express their displeasure or simply their opinion. Do I think it is morally correct to burn our flag or the Bible? Not at all, but if the Bill of Rights or the Constitution gives people that right, then they have that right.

Today, though, we are told that we should not burn a Qur'an. Why? Because it will upset Muslims. I can appreciate the fact that they will not like it. However, unlike authentic Christians who become offended when forced to take down the Ten Commandments or because of something else, we do *not* riot about it. We do not gather as a mob and simply chant some asinine statement pumping our fists in the air. Further, we do not spit on people, nor do we become physically combative when things do not go our way.

Muslims do these things. They are prone to gather in mobs and work themselves up to a lather that literally begs for a reason to start beating on someone. It has happened too many times in parts of Europe, and now we are beginning to see it happen in Dearborn, MI.

The people of the United States have long participated in peaceful protests. Sometimes – usually due to the criminal element – those peaceful protests become riots and the police need to be called in. However, that is not always the case. Can someone show me where Muslims have gathered to protest something when it did not become riotous?

Today's Muslim seems to have a penchant for violence, and while we have "moderate" Muslims who beg to differ, the reality is that by and large, when Muslims protest something, they do it in force and en masse. They are not kidding about it, and essentially, they are holding that area of the world hostage until they get what they want.

This has created a "thug" mentality among many Muslims. This is why they can now spit on a videographer who is doing nothing more than attending one of "their" festivals and recording what he sees. This thug mentality has quickly spread so that it is becoming the norm.

A short while ago, I discussed the billboard that my wife and I saw on the way to her class in San Francisco; the one that advertises Islam as a religion of peace. When you go to the Website listed on the billboard, it provides details about the peaceful religion of Islam. It talks about Muhammad and the fact that he was not the messiah. It also speaks of Islam's messiah that apparently was already here.

It would seem, then, that this particular Islamic sect differs from the more mainstream and well-known Islam that everyone hears about because of their actions. Does this peaceful sect of Islam even have a chance against their murderous and warring brothers? It's certainly doubtful.

The more important question, as I believe I asked last time, is, why aren't these peaceful Muslims standing in the gap between their murderous counterparts and the rest of the world? If these peaceful Muslims truly want peace, a good place to start would be to stand opposed to radical Islam. I don't see them doing that, and all their "education" in the world isn't going to change that.

If a gang of thugs slowly began moving into my neighborhood, I would do something about it. I would first of all increase my vigilance, and whenever I saw something that was not within the confines of the law, I would notify the police. I would also do what I could to ensure that my family was protected as much as possible.

The bad thing about thugs is that they normally only respond to force. They see anything less than this as cowardice. Unfortunately, this is what many Muslims have become. I'm not even sure that there is such a thing as a "moderate" Muslim anymore. Just lately, one of the men who was considered by our government to be "moderate" turned out to be a full-blown radical, and he was born in America!

I think it is extremely important to be aware of what is going on in the world. We may or may not be able to change it, but to be unaware of what is happening is the worst possible thing. By being unaware, you may believe that you can move through life blissfully ignorant to all the dangers, but normally, it is only a matter of time before those dangers overtake you and you are sunk.

I know that we live in an area where rattlesnakes are common. You never know where one will pop up and so it is advisable to always be conscious of the fact that one might be under every rock you pass.

A few summers ago, my wife and I were jogging along the bike path not far from our home. It was a nice trail and since it was covered with asphalt, you didn't have to worry so much about twisting your ankle like you would if running in a field.

At any rate, we were busy jogging and talking, and I wasn't really paying attention to my own surroundings. Out of the corner of my eye, I sensed movement and then heard what sounded like paper shaking in the wind. It took about two or three seconds before I realized that just in front of me to my right was a huge rattler! Frankly, I didn't think I was capable of jumping as high as I did! We ran about ten yards away then stopped and looked back.

What had happened was that just as we rounded the bend of one turn, the snake had been in the middle of the path, crossing it. As we approached, it of course felt threatened and started rattling for us. It was not in a coiled position at that point, which was good, because rattlers cannot strike unless coiled, but as it moved off the path, it stretched its neck back over itself in our direction.

As we stood away from it, it was still rattling! Yes, it freaked me out. I hate rattlesnakes because they can kill. Since that time, I have been very wary of jogging along that path since it runs right through a green belt. A green belt here in California is a place that is considered a sort of sanctuary for animals. No building allowed, etc. There are plenty of places for a snake to hide.

Whenever we go down there, I am always aware of the potential of running across a snake. We've seen other things down there as well, such as plenty of wild turkeys, coyotes, owls, and more. I would never again go to that area blindly assuming that the snakes are gone or that they will not hurt me. If a rattler feels cornered, it will strike.

But that's the animal kingdom. In the Islamic world, many Muslims have grown to the point of believing that as long as they push hard enough, they will eventually get what they want. The U.K. has obliged. Dearborn, MI is obliging, and other areas of the world are doing the same.

However, some are pushing back. France has passed a law against wearing a full burka that covers the face. Other countries are saying "enough" to the constant Muslim immigration and demands put forth by Muslim activists.

Years ago, I tried to envision what the end times would look like before Jesus returned. I knew it would be bad, but it was really difficult to pin things down specifically. We know that Paul and Peter tell us that people will become extremely self-centered, demanding, egotistical, and progressively more evil. That much is and has been happening.

What we did not really know is that Islam would seem to be playing such a huge role in bringing all of that about. This is sad to say, but in many ways, Islam has provoked people to action because people have had enough. We do not want to be told that we must respect the religion of Islam when they show absolutely no willingness to respect anyone else's religious beliefs.

We have grown tired of people demanding special favors when no one else receives them. Just recently, a Police Captain in Tulsa was suspended without pay for two weeks because he refused to attend a Law Enforcement Appreciation Day held by a local mosque. As it turns out, there was some proselytizing going on at the event. The captain refused to attend on the grounds of his own religious convictions and was eventually suspended.

ACT! for America asks the question, would the same thing have happened had the event been at a local synagogue? Good question. I wonder if the same thing would have happened had the sponsoring organization been a church.

Think of it. Because a police officer refused on religious grounds to attend what turned out to be an indoctrination event held by local Muslims, he was suspended. Where is the ACLU? Had the event been held at a church or synagogue and he failed to attend, he either would not have been suspended, or if so, the ACLU would have certainly gotten involved.

Folks, as we move closer to the time of the coming Tribulation, things are going to get worse in many ways. Right now, we are experiencing a financial crisis in this nation that Mr. Obama has done nothing to eliminate. In fact, he has made it far worse.

Food prices are continuing to rise, as are gas prices. We are at war in Afghanistan and Libya, in spite of what this Administration would like us to believe, and even though Mr. Obama is going to begin pulling 10,000 troops out now and 30,000 by the end of 2012, I believe, under the circumstances, these numbers are too high and too soon. Too many believe that if we just pull out of Afghanistan, all will be right with the world because radical Islam will leave us alone. No, they will simply see it as our "giving up" rather than anything else.

So what can we do? Well, obviously, the first thing is to be sure that you are, in fact, in relationship with Jesus. Make sure you have salvation. That is number one. Number two is similar to it. Make sure that you are submitting yourself to Him daily. Number three, seek His wisdom as you face the uncertainties of life. Four, be as prepared as you possibly can as if you were going on an extended camping trip. You may need to grow your own vegetables, stock up on food and water, and drive less by combining multiple trips into one. Ride a bike, not only for exercise, but to use less gas and depend less on your vehicle.

We are not sunk. God will protect us and provide for our daily bread. Above all things, as evil vomits itself onto the land, we can and should know that God loves us and has great things in store for us – in the next life. He is with us now – absolutely – and He will never leave or forsake us. Can we trust someone like that? You bet!

It may appear as though Islam is winning the war. I hate it when I hear that we are at war with Islam. That's not quite true. Yes, in one sense, we are at war; however, they fired the first shot. They incited this war.

However, we cannot allow ourselves to simply focus on this war of ideologies. If we do, we can easily become sidetracked. We must focus on the fact that there are individuals within Islam whom the Lord will save. If we see them as the enemy, we have lost because we will fail to do the most important thing that we should be involved in doing: evangelizing the lost.

Say it with me: *"The Lord is my Protector. He is my Guide. While Islam threatens my very existence, He will not leave or forsake me. In fact, He will give me the wisdom necessary to fight the way He would fight."*

Think about the fact that an ideological war is going on and the best way to fight it still is through prayer. That is difficult but I must remember that our fight is not against flesh and blood, but against powers and principalities.

The devil would like me to focus on the individuals within Islam as objects of hate. God wants me to focus on them as objects of His love. In these dark days, I need to be more of a prayer warrior than ever before. God has already won the war. I want to ensure that I do not be the reason a battle is lost.

Chapter 16
Self and Idolatry

I have been reading through Isaiah, and this morning Chapters 43 and 44 were on the schedule. What is interesting to me is how God takes the time to fully explain Himself and His positions, as well as the ironic ways that humans often see the world.

Isaiah 44 speaks about – among other things – idolatry. Verses 6 – 8 clearly lay the foundation for God's argument that follows.

> *"'I am the first and I am the last,*
> *And there is no God besides Me.*
> *7 'Who is like Me? Let him proclaim and declare it;*
> *Yes, let him recount it to Me in order,*

From the time that I established the ancient nation.
And let them declare to them the things that are coming
And the events that are going to take place.
8 'Do not tremble and do not be afraid;
Have I not long since announced it to you and declared it?
And you are My witnesses.
Is there any God besides Me,
Or is there any other Rock?
I know of none.'"

Well? Any takers? Bueller?

You have to appreciate the fact that God is so straightforward. Here, He states clearly that there is no God besides Him. None. Nada. Zilch. Zippo. Some, by the way, use this to "prove" that Jesus is not God. Just the opposite. It proves He is God, since He also states that "I and my Father are One" (John 10:30), as well as other things. The fascinating thing is that the Bible is a unit, and therefore should be allowed to interpret itself. Many try, but they seem to do a half-baked job at best. That's another blog though.

For now, I want to continue with Isaiah 44. After God boldly claims that there is no other god besides Him, He then moves on to scenarios in which people find themselves. The irony of those situations is that these people do not realize their own stupidity.

Verse 9 tells us, *"Those who fashion a graven image are all of them futile, and their precious things are of no profit; even their own witnesses fail to see or know, so that they will be put to shame."* Amazing, isn't it? What people fail to see is that either they or some craftsperson create an image that people worship. The image has no value, except the inherent value of the material itself. Those graven images can do absolutely nothing for the person, yet people routinely believe that they can.

If you take the time to do even a cursory search across the 'Net, you will find a plethora of places that sell crystals and other "healing" products. You can purchase crystal jewelry, crystal beads, crystals by location, by material, by size or shape, and by color. You can shop at Wicca stores where you may purchase any number of items that are designed to help you overcome aspects of life that you find troubling. Of course, Tarot Cards are always there to help you understand all the mysteries of life too.

People deliberately place their faith in these things, but God says – in verse 9 – that these things have no value to help. They are futile and essentially worthless. In the end, the person who trusts in those things will be put to shame. Imagine the people in hell who will spend eternity kicking themselves for their stupidity when they placed faith in some graven image.

Probably the saddest part of this entire chapter of Isaiah is toward the end, when God takes pains to explain how a man will buy a piece of wood and use part of it for a fire in his hearth. There, he will bake bread to feed himself. With the other part of the same piece of wood, he will craft an image that he can worship. Is this not insane?

I absolutely love the way God makes this so brutally clear in verses 16 – 17. *"Half of it he burns in the fire; over this half he eats meat as he roasts a roast and is satisfied. He also warms himself and says, 'Aha! I am warm, I have seen the fire.' 17 But the rest of it he makes into a god, his graven image. He falls down before it and worships; he also prays to it and says, 'Deliver me, for you are my god.'"*

Is this asinine or what? We read this and think of an idiot savant who cannot distinguish truth from error. From the same piece of wood, a man cooks his food and creates a god. How absurd is that? When he finishes eating, he turns to the other part of the same piece of wood and announces that IT (the wood) is his god! How ludicrous, yet here we are in 2011 and we do the exact same thing!

We have crystals hanging from our rear-view mirrors, we carry them around our necks or wrists, and we place our trust in them to save us or to protect us. How many people do you know that carry a "good luck" charm? If they lose it, they are beside themselves with worry because they have lost their protection!

The person who creates or purchases something that he/she can put his/her faith in is summed up by God in verses 19-20 of Isaiah 44. *"No one recalls, nor is there knowledge or understanding to say, 'I have burned half of it in the fire and also have baked bread over its coals. I roast meat and eat it. Then I make the rest of it into an abomination, I fall down before a block of wood!' 20 He feeds on ashes; a deceived heart has turned him aside. And he cannot deliver himself, nor say, 'Is there not a lie in my right hand?'"*

So in spite of the fact that the person in the above scenario understands that he took a piece of wood, used half of it to cook his food and used the remaining half to create a god to worship, this same person seems completely unaware of the fact that he has created his own god, which started off as a piece of wood that baked his bread! In fact, it remained a piece of wood. It never changed from being a piece of wood to something else. He (or a craftsperson) simply changed what the wood looked like outwardly, but that did nothing to change the fact that it was and remains a piece of wood.

The man never stopped to say to himself, "Hey wait a minute. I took part of this piece of wood and cooked my food. I then took the other part and created a god I worship. What is wrong with this picture?" The man never stopped to realize what he was doing. Had he done so, he likely would have said something like, *"This is ridiculous! How can the same piece of wood be used for cooking and to become my god?"*

I appreciate the last question in the quoted verses above: Is there not a lie in my right hand? No one gets to that point, though, do we? Think of the situation with Paul in Acts 17. Beginning in verse 16, we read of Paul's view of Athens and how disheartened he became because of all the idolatry. You'll recall that this is where Paul presented his sermon on Mars Hill, calling attention to the fact that these people even had an idol dedicated to the "unknown" god. Paul used that as his introduction to point to Jesus, who was unknown to them.

How about the situation recorded in Acts 19, where Paul heads to Ephesus and because of his preaching, not only were many saved, but these saved individuals took their charms, their idols, their magic books and everything connected with them and burned them in front of everyone. While Paul was there, not only did he preach the gospel, but people were healed and demons were cast out.

Of course, when the people of Ephesus in Acts 19 burned all their magic books and idols, the craftsmen – led by Demetrius – became upset because they saw their livelihood going down the drain. They got together and protested in anger, and this created a problem for Paul.

People want to protect their businesses, and imagine if the average person did not believe in the idols of today. There would be far fewer New Age bookstores selling their wares.

In this same section of Scripture, we learn about the Seven Sons of Sceva. This is a very interesting section. Like many others, these guys had seen Paul casting out demons and healing the sick. Remember, this area was known for its occult beliefs and practices. These seven men thought, *"Hey, that's cool. We haven't tried casting out demons in Jesus' Name before. Let's give that a shot!"* So they did and were met with heavy resistance from the demon. The "self" within these seven brothers thought for sure they could handle any demons with this newfound alternative to the way they normally handled things like this. They were brutally wrong.

In fact, the text specifically states (when they tried casting out demons like Paul did), *"I recognize Jesus, and I know about Paul, but who are you?"* (v. 15). You have to love that! These demons actually knew Jesus (of course, since He was/is God!), and they had heard about Paul (proof that neither demons nor Satan can be everywhere at once) – I guess news travels among the demonic hordes – but they had no clue about these seven guys! One thing the demon did know was that these seven brothers had no power or ability over it, and it was going to prove that point. The demon did, leaving the brothers bleeding, wounded, and naked as they fled the house where the possessed man lived. Interestingly, the text tells us that it was one demon ("the evil spirit").

In Isaiah 44, God is speaking to Israel. He is warning them that they must put aside the idols that they have faith in and turn unreservedly to Him, the only God. During this chapter, God announces how much He loves Israel and how He has forgiven them and how they will one day realize the honor of being part of Israel.

Verse 5 tells us of this future picture of Jews who will love being part of the nation that God created. As His Remnant of the future, they will delight in that honor. *"This one will say, 'I am the LORD'S'; And that one will call on the name of Jacob; And another will write on his hand, 'Belonging to the LORD,' And will name Israel's name with honor."*

Generally, I'm against tattoos; however, if I were Jewish and a believer, I might make an exception. I would find it a considerable honor to tattoo the phrase *"Belonging to the LORD"* somewhere on my right hand.

I marvel at how Isaiah mixes the past with the future. God is constantly comparing and contrasting Israel of old with the purified Israel of the future. The Israel of old is the Israel that worshiped anything to gain something, in spite of the reality that no idol ever did anything good for them.

The Israel of the future is the Israel that exists during the Millennial reign of Jesus. They will serve Him gladly, and the other nations that are to be included in this Millennial Kingdom will yearn to attach themselves to Jews, unlike today, where Jews are defamed at every turn, even by other Jews.

Idols can do nothing good for a person. Yet we see a growing movement within society that endeavors to enhance idolatry, bringing it into the mainstream.

There are strands of the Emergent Church that are aligning itself with aspects of idolatry. They use prayer beads or crystals as a "help" in prayer, but in reality, all they are doing is crossing the line from worshiping God to trusting idols.

The truth is that many within Christendom today are changing the way they look at the Bible, at God, and at the gospel. Those within the Emergent Church (which is really the secular New Age cloned in religious garb) have manufactured a type of idolatrous "Christianity" that allows them to use their idols of choice while continuing to believe that they are practicing Christianity.

However, from God's Word there can be no doubt that idolatry is an anathema to God. It doesn't matter if it is simply a "good luck" charm or a full-blown crystal hanging around our neck. The end result is that the use of crystals is nothing more than idolatry.

As Christians, we certainly need to take the time to assess our lives. What are we treating as if it was an idol? What are we substituting for God, which, of course, is no substitute at all, except in our minds?

If we have idols in our life, we are no better off than the person in Isaiah 44 who falls down before a piece of wood. While nothing good will come of it, plenty of bad will.

Our world is on the fast track toward one-worldism. A growing global movement is underway to become united as one people, with one person who will lead us. This is no time for Christians to have any idols in their life. All must be surrendered to God. Maybe as a reminder, it might be a good idea to carry a card with the phrase *"Belonging to the LORD"* on it. This at least will help us remember that we no longer belong to ourselves.

If the Lord is going to protect us and provide for us in the coming days, it is extremely important that nothing in our life is kept from Him. We must surrender all things – including anything that can even be construed as an idol – in order that He will have His full sway in and over our lives. This should be done for no other reason than for His glory.

I don't want to ever hear God say of me, "He feeds on ashes; a deceived heart has turned him aside. And he cannot deliver himself, nor say, *'Is there not a lie in my right hand?'*" Do you?

Chapter 17
Self and False Prophets

Certainly, most know by now of a man named Harold Camping, president of Family Radio. He became famous for, among other things, predicting the Lord's return *twice* and being wrong about it. The last time, he said the Lord would return May 21, 2011 at 6:00pm. He was obviously wrong. He was not deterred, though, because when that weekend came and went, he simply said what I and many others knew he would say. He offered that the Lord *had indeed* returned, but *spiritually*. He then modified his prediction by stating that this October 21, 2011 was really the end. Really. *Honest.* It is going to happen.

A few weeks ago as I write this, Mr. Camping suffered a stroke. Everyone said he was fine except for some slurred speech. They said he was improving and would soon continue his broadcasts. Today his radio show has been canceled because apparently, Mr. Camping's voice is gone. Is this coincidence, or did the Lord take the time to judge Mr. Camping's erroneous predictions?

I'm sure you have your own opinion about this, but I firmly believe that the Lord took this time to remove Mr. Camping's voice because for too long he has been in a position where he literally speaks for the Lord, yet what he preaches is – *at best* – a twisted version of biblical truth. Therefore, it is *not* truth.

For some time, Mr. Camping has taught his followers numerous doctrines that, in my opinion, are without Scriptural basis. For instance, he came around to believing that the Lord had specifically told him the Church Age is over. Because of this belief, he goes on to assert that people should actually *leave* their churches and form what he has termed "fellowships." This is nothing more than groups of people meeting without any type of authority over them, except, of course, the Bible.

This means that there is no trained pastor or overseer, one who is capable of rightly dividing the Word of truth. Obviously, in such a situation error can easily rise to the surface, and with no checks or balances the entire group can succumb to the error taught by one individual in that particular "fellowship."

Mr. Camping has stated that the Holy Spirit is no longer operating within the local churches, which is why people need to leave them. This is directly opposed to Scripture because we know that the Holy Spirit indwells each and every authentic believer from the moment of salvation (cf. Luke 17:21; Acts 17:24). The Holy Spirit indwells the *believer* and it is the believers that make up the Church. Together, all believers form the Church, which is the Bride of Christ.

It follows, then, according to Camping's teachings, that *if* the Holy Spirit is no longer working within the local church assembly, then it is impossible for people to be saved in those assemblies. This is the reason that people need to leave them, according to Camping. Salvation is no longer found within the church, but outside of it.

Of course, in this it is obvious that Camping makes no distinction between the visible and invisible Church. The visible church is what we see with people saying they are Christians and may not be. They may merely be professing Christians. So when we see a group of people worshiping on Sunday mornings, we are seeing the visible church. We do not know who is and who is not truly and authentically saved.

Only the truly authentic believers make up the invisible Church, and we cannot see into people's hearts to know the truth of their salvation. Because of this, it is impossible to judge each congregation of people to determine who is and who is not saved. Camping makes no distinction, indicating that the church – the local body of people – should be abandoned.

Mr. Camping also denies the doctrine of eternal damnation, something that Jesus obviously taught in numerous places throughout the gospels; yet in spite of this, His Words are often misrepresented by people who do not want to believe that there is such a thing as eternal torment of the lost.

While it is a doctrine that often repels, that in and of itself does not mean it is not true or is somehow humanly created. Instead of teaching that there will be people who suffer for all of eternity, folks like Camping prefer to teach that those who are not saved are simply annihilated out of existence. It should be noted that cults like Jehovah's Witnesses teach the same thing.

The Bible is very clear when it speaks of the second death, which is not annihilation, but an actual, "living" death that goes on for all eternity. We read about references to this second death in Re 20:10, 14, 15; 21:8; Mt 25:41, and elsewhere. People like to try to prove that this second death is merely a fading out of existence, but from the descriptions provided in Revelation alone, it is clear that this second death is an ongoing, eternal process.

"And the devil who deceived them was thrown into the lake of fire and brimstone, where the beast and the false prophet are also; and they will be tormented day and night forever and ever" (Revelation 20:10).

In Matthew 25:45, Jesus Himself speaks of the same thing: *"Then He will also say to those on His left, 'Depart from Me, accursed ones, into the eternal fire which has been prepared for the devil and his angels.'"*

Note that in both cases, we are told that this torment goes on forever *and* ever. Jesus calls this the "eternal fire." It is difficult – when Scripture is allowed to interpret itself – to come to any other conclusion than that people (along with the devil and his angels) who are imprisoned in the Lake of Fire will experience the torment of that fire for all of eternity. Note that the text specifically states that it is eternal, as opposed to limited by *time*. This should obviously be taken as *unending*.

These are just a few of the teachings that Mr. Camping has taught from the platform of his own radio program. This type of error should not be tolerated, but since Camping is his own boss, he is not going to be corrected by anyone since there is no one who is over him or at least on par with him who can correct him.

In 1994, Camping predicted that the world would come to an end then. When it did not, he asked a lot of questions and then apparently realized that his math was wrong. So, he worked out the problem and arrived at a new date, May 21, 2011. That date came and went and nothing happened. Now, Camping says that the real end of the world is going to happen on October 21, 2011, but he does not feel the need to discuss it.

Frankly, after May 21st came and went, I posted on my blog that unless the Lord saw a reason to not do this, Camping should be taken from this planet. That may sound like demagoguery, but the reality is that I'm concerned for the people he continues to lead astray. I also stated on my blog that I pray that if I am ever disposed to make the type of doctrinal mistakes that Camping has made, I would hope the Lord would take me home long before that!

On June 13, 2011, it was reported that Harold Camping had suffered a stroke. It has affected his speech, and in spite of the fact that his wife and others were saying he would recover, as of this writing, he remains hospitalized and his voice is now gone. Is this simply a coincidence? I don't believe so.

I fully believe that the Lord's extended grace to Mr. Camping has given out. This is not to say that the Lord has deserted Mr. Camping. It means that the Lord has now moved to protect what is left of His Name, something that Mr. Camping has essentially dragged through the mud with his false prophesies.

It remains to be seen what will happen with Mr. Camping, and certainly his life is in the Lord's hands. My prayer is that the Lord will graciously open Mr. Camping's eyes to the error of his ways and to the truth of God's Word.

It was recently announced that Mr. Camping's program is over. It will be replaced with other programming simply because without his voice, Mr. Camping cannot teach anything, much less some of the error that he has been teaching over the years.

Mr. Camping has erred due to Self. He placed himself in a position where he answered to no one. He is "self-taught" regarding the Bible.

While it is not wrong to study the Bible on your own, it is extremely important to at least be under the tutelage of others who are far more well-versed in Scripture. Mr. Camping spent his life as an engineer and studied the Bible without benefit of people who could have addressed his errors before they became things that identified his ministry.

Camping chose not to do this, starting a ministry that has grown tremendously; yet because of it, he has spread his error to the millions of people who routinely listen to and believe what he teaches.

Self can be so deceptive. We see this clearly in Mr. Camping's case, and it seems clear enough that God Himself has had enough of Camping's error, taught as truth.

False prophets are extremely dangerous because they have an air of authority that people often are unwilling to question. False prophets believe their teachings to be true because there are no checks and balances for them. They are on their own, and that's fine with them.

Harold Camping is a false prophet because he has *prophesied* things about God that turned out to be *false*. If this had been done during the time of Israel in the Old Testament, he would have been taken outside the camp and stoned to death because he would have been attributing to God what did not come from God.

Harold Camping is not the only person who has taught things based on God's Word that turned out to be false. Does this mean that the entire Premillennial viewpoint of the end times is false? Not at all. It means that Camping and others like him essentially claim that *their* teaching is accurately based on Scripture when it is obviously not the case.

Because of Camping's false teachings, people donated their entire savings to Family Radio so that he could get the word out about the

May 21st date. Some quit their jobs and spent what they believed would be their remaining days passing out leaflets. They are individually responsible for the fact that they did not study the Bible on their own or seek the opinion of others who were more well-versed in knowledge of Scripture than they *and* Harold Camping are.

When we begin to doubt certain orthodox doctrines of Scripture, like eternal punishment or the idea that the Holy Spirit is still working in the church, we leave ourselves open to even greater error as time goes on. This is what has happened with Harold Camping's program in which people would call in and ask him questions about the Bible.

As I've noted previously, Self can be a very heady cocktail. It continually reveals itself as an entity that cares only about what makes it happy. As in the case of Harold Camping, he wound up deliberately positioning himself as a "standalone" Bible teacher under no one else's authority. Therefore, it was simply him and the Holy Spirit. There is nothing necessarily wrong with that, but we should always be open to critique, help, and teaching from others because other people help keep us balanced in our approach to the Bible. Those who are their own firebrands wind up either burning themselves, others, or both. Harold Camping is simply proof of that one point.

Chapter 18
Self and False Messiahs

Maitreya – the coming world teacher, as the New Age believes – is here. He appeared to 6,000 in Africa in June of 1988. He has made other appearances as well.

In listening to many individuals on videos (available on Youtube.com) who testify about Maitreya, the sense that we get is that a particular religion one belongs to does not matter. What matters is what we do with the teachings of Maitreya. These folks are also quite sure that this is exactly what Jesus taught as well.

The main push, if you will, of Maitreya has to do with sharing. According to followers, Maitreya teaches that we should share what we have with all of humanity. One woman on a video said that this is what we do with members of our nuclear family, so should we not also do this with all humanity since we are all connected through our humanity?

Maitreya's main concern seems to be feeding the world. While this was not Jesus' main concern, it was certainly one of His concerns. He fed thousands on numerous occasions. Did Maitreya? Jesus did so because it would have been impossible for them to all leave His presence, walk to town and purchase their own food. They were there listening to Him, so He fed them, caring for their physical need of hunger in order to meet their spiritual thirst as well.

Maitreya did not do this during his appearance in June of 1988. He taught that we should feed one another and take care of one another. Of course, interestingly enough, Raj Patel is a man whose main goal is to feed the world. Many are coming round to believe that Patel is Maitreya. To date, he has not officially denied, nor has he officially proclaimed it (as far as I know).

Patel feels a very real concern for the hungry people of this world, and he speaks out against the corporate greed that makes it nearly impossible to feed all the people of the world. What is interesting, in my opinion, is that Patel is thoroughly involved in a subject that all can relate to, yet at the same time is not overtly political. What I mean by that is that when we speak of people starving throughout the world, our hearts normally go out to them. It is not so much a political issue as it is a social one.

Hunger crosses the board and shows no preference for ethnicity or culture. If you happen to live in a part of the world affected by drought, a lack of food can certainly affect you. Unfortunately, that is often the case in third world countries, but not always. Russia's recent severe drought that negatively impacted their wheat crop is a case in point. The entire world is affected by that shortage.

Hunger is not like the subject of abortion, for instance. No one stands on the "I think people should be allowed to starve to death! They should be allowed to do what they want with their bodies!" side, while others stand directly opposed to them. So, in that way, the entire world supports the idea that no one should go hungry. Even corporations can get into the "giving" spirit by helping those who do not have much to at least have something. It's a win-win situation for everyone, especially "Maitreya" Patel. Who would dare stand against what Patel is doing? Who would stand opposed to Maitreya, when his biggest concern is to ensure that all people of the world are fed?

Since 1988, Maitreya has allegedly appeared several times. As quickly as he arrives, he is gone; there to provide a message of hope and direction, then moving on, allowing that message to sink in.

The unsurprising fact of the matter is the belief that this Maitreya (whom many refer to as "Jesus") is someone who transcends all religious lines and barriers. This is actually not true. Everything the Maitreya teaches is fully in line with the New Age belief system. Though he does not outwardly reject it, Maitreya does not include orthodox Christianity because of the fact that orthodox Christianity and New Age tenets simply are not capable of co-existing, much to the chagrin of the people who have a bumper sticker that says otherwise.

The tragedy, though, is that people truly believe that this Maitreya is the guy for this generation. He is teaching that we need to join together to accomplish the goals of feeding the hungry and treating all people as our brothers and sisters, yet at the same time, he teaches that we must realize our own deity. Where have we heard that before? This is eerily familiar to the Tower of Babel in Genesis 11, where Nimrod gathered all people together as one in order to take control of their future. By building a tower that would reach to the heavens, they would become united in practice and goal. In doing so, they would release their own inner deity in order to be able to accomplish the very goal that stood before them. Even God said that once they accomplished that, there would be nothing they could not do (cf. Genesis 11:1-9).

Here's the problem, though. Aside from being overtly New Age ("I am god, you are god, we are all gods"), there is a much larger issue at hand here. It is an issue that Jesus Himself thoroughly warned us about. Because of that, we have no excuse. That is only part of the reason Jesus warned us, though. The other reason He warned us was so that we would actually heed His message.

What was/is His message in this case? Simply put, Jesus warned – in the Olivet Discourse – that when He returned, every eye would see Him. Let's look at the text, shall we? He first tells His disciples the following:

"Then if anyone says to you, 'Behold, here is the Christ,' or 'There He is,' do not believe him. For false Christs and false prophets will arise and will show great signs and wonders, so as to mislead, if possible, even the elect. Behold, I have told you in advance. So if they say to you, 'Behold, He is in the wilderness,' do not go out, or, 'Behold, He is in the inner rooms,' do not believe them. For just as the lightning comes from the east and flashes even to the west, so will the coming of the Son of Man be. Wherever the corpse is, there the vultures will gather." (Matthew 24:23-28)

Correct me if I'm wrong, but that is exactly what people said when Maitreya appeared to the 6,000 people in June of 1988 in a small village in Africa. During that event (which was photographed, but not video-taped), we see a man in Middle Eastern garb walking through the crowd. He told the leader (a woman who began a church in the village), as he paced off a distance, that people should run the length of that path then return to her, and their problems would be solved.

Since that time, thousands have done just that. People from all walks of life – Buddhists, Hindus, professing Christians, and others – have walked the path (reminds me of walking the labyrinth) to find release from the problems that ail them physically as well as emotionally or socially.

As far as signs and wonders go, this one was not that great, yet it caused people to obey and to put faith in walking the path. They come from all over in order to follow in the footsteps of Maitreya. The woman leader now says she hears "his" voice all the time, very loudly. She sees things through a type of screen that allows her to know what needs to happen in a person's life. Sounds a bit demonic to me.

So we have a situation in which a mysterious man appears, speaks to the crowd in perfect Swahili (without an accent), shares some insights, and then literally disappears from them. Because of that event, thousands are told "he is there!" or "he is here!" They then go there or here in an effort to find him or to gain what he allegedly left behind. But didn't Jesus say that just as lightning flashes from the east to the west, so will His return be? What does that mean except that the heavenly light show will announce His return boldly?

The next section of verses – 29-31 – tell us what Jesus' actual return to this planet will look like, and it is not too difficult to imagine it based on Jesus' description of that event.

"But immediately after the tribulation of those days THE SUN WILL BE DARKENED, AND THE MOON WILL NOT GIVE ITS LIGHT, AND THE STARS WILL FALL from the sky, and the powers of the heavens will be shaken. **And then the sign of the Son of Man will appear in the sky, and then all the tribes of the earth will mourn, and they will see the SON OF MAN COMING ON THE CLOUDS OF THE SKY** *with power and great glory. And He will send forth His angels with A GREAT*

TRUMPET and THEY WILL GATHER TOGETHER His elect from the four winds, from one end of the sky to the other (emphasis added)."

This particular description is far different from the description of Maitreya's appearance, isn't it? On the one hand, we have Maitreya appearing to a group of 6,000 in Africa. He's here, then "poof!" he's gone. Did every eye see him? Did he come in the clouds? Nope.

On the other hand, Jesus specifically states that when He returns, the entire world will notice. Why is that? It is simply due to the event itself as it unfolds:

1. *The sun will go dark*
2. *The moon will have no light to reflect*
3. *The stars will fall from the sky*
4. *The powers of the heavens will be shaken*

Take a look at those four things. That is describing tremendous upheaval in the heavens! The sun will go dark? Yikes! Nothing for the moon to reflect? Stars will fall from the sky? The powers of heaven will shake! Yes, all of that.

That is some fanfare we are reading about. This is like the race cars revving their engines just prior to the green flag. I've talked to people who have attended events like the Indy 500 or Talladega and they tell me that the sound of the cars' engines is so powerful, it can actually be felt in a person's chest. Imagine that.

Jesus is saying that just prior to His physical return, the heavens are going to get the world's attention. Now, if those four things happen, where do you think people will be looking? Exactly, they will be looking up.

Following those four things, the world will see Jesus coming on the clouds in the sky with what? Power and great glory! Amen!

No one who is alive on this planet will miss seeing that event take place. Yet, when Maitreya appeared in June of 1988, only 6,000 people saw him. The sun did not go dark. The moon continued to reflect the sun's light. No stars fell from the heavens (that anyone reported), and there was nothing going on in the heavens that would cause people to take notice.

Jesus promised that when He returns, the entire world will see His return! So on three counts here, we have Maitreya failing miserably. First, he appears literally in "the desert" or "wilderness," and second, the entire world did not see his appearance – unless of course the entire world happened to see the story that was written about the event several days or weeks later. Third, this Maitreya seems only concerned about people's physical welfare. He does not distinguish between the religions because in essence, except for Christianity (and Judaism from which it sprang), all other religions are from the same source. That source is Satan himself. No one likes to hear that about their own personal belief system, but if people would simply take the time to compare their religious beliefs with Christianity, they would clearly see the difference. As it is, most people think they know what Christianity is and therefore do not need to study it on their own.

A good portion of the world (but not all of it) knows about Maitreya because Benjamin Creme (Share International) keeps his name out there. I fully believe there will be many other false Christs as well. There already have been, and some of them are still living today, still claiming to be "the son of God." They can't all be right. In fact, none of them are right. They are all liars and false prophets seeking to control the masses and deceive them into remaining on the broad path that leads to destruction (cf. Matthew 7:13-14). Their time is short, though, and the demons that animate and instill them with lies that seem to be truth are moving ahead with great speed to destroy any faith in the God of the Bible that people possess. They will ultimately fail, of course.

You may be one of them. You may think that this Maitreya (or someone else) has the keys to life eternal. You may fully believe that what you hear from your "savior" is truth, but if you would stop long enough to compare what your "savior" is teaching with all the rest, and then compare that with the teachings of Jesus, you would find that something is completely out of kilter.

The truth is that you really do not have much time. First, you do not know when your death will occur – no one does. Second, you do not know when the real Jesus will return. Yet you are content to accept the lies that are presented to you as truth because of how those lies make you feel.

Jesus Himself gave you at least two measuring rods to determine truth when it comes to the individuals who are touted as the "messiah." How do these individuals measure up to His Word and how do the inner leadings of the Holy Spirit testify with respect to their teachings? I have shown you that these individuals fail in at least three ways. Yet you persist in hanging onto your beliefs because the idea of submitting yourself to the only God of the universe is galling to you. No one likes to submit.

Instead, you would rather be as you are and simply follow someone with whom you already agree. That requires no change at all.

Okay, so let's take a look at that for a quick moment. Maitreya essentially preaches that we should care for one another. Many people preach that. What makes Maitreya so special? Could it be he "appeared" and "disappeared" instantaneously, therefore he surrounded himself with an aura that all other preachers of "save the earth – feed the hungry" policies do not have? In other words, his alleged supernatural appearance, along with his message to care for one another, made him stand out not because of his message, but because of the way he came and went.

But what about a person's *soul*? What about eternity? What about all the other things Jesus preached about? Does all of this get swept away simply because the main thrust of Maitreya's message is feeding the hungry and he introduced that message with a bit of flare?

I also believe it is very important to do whatever we can to feed the poor, care for the sick, and make people's lives more comfortable. However, in the end, none of that gives them what they truly need: salvation for their souls.

Feeding a person cannot provide salvation. It can only give them enough energy to hear the message of the gospel, but in itself cannot provide true salvation.

Maitreya did not take the message far enough because he can't. Like all false prophets/messiahs, he does not want people saved. He is a modern-day Nimrod of Genesis 11. He does not want people to come to know the Author of Life. He is handing out the false hope that if we will simply provide food for the hungry and care for the sick, then we will have what he implies is salvation.

Jesus absolutely took the time to feed the hungry and heal the sick and infirm. He did it to call attention to the fact that by ourselves, we as people are not whole. The miracles of feeding the five or ten thousand, healing the sick, and even raising the dead were done not as an end in and of themselves. They were done to call attention to the fact that He was/is God in the flesh and also to help people understand that they need what only He can provide.

Maitreya's message is half-baked. Feed the hungry. That's a great idea and something that authentic Christians have been involved in doing for centuries. The difference between Maitreya and his followers and Jesus and His followers is that authentic Christians know that feeding people and caring for their needs is merely a way to help them understand the greatest need they have, which cannot be met with physical food and clothing. The greatest need all people have is salvation, and this salvation only comes through Jesus.

Maitreya doesn't preach that because he can't. Apollo C. Quiboloy doesn't preach that because he can't. False prophets/messiahs preach a truth mixed with error, which of course is no truth at all. Like a good magician, all these people do is redirect. They teach people that the most important thing they can do is feed the hungry, or, essentially, serve others.

While this is a part of the Jesus' message, it is not the entirety of it. The gospel has a message that every individual will have to respond to. It begins with a question: who do you think Jesus is?

Either Jesus is God the Son, or He isn't. If He is, then to ignore His entire message, or truncate it like Maitreya and others do, robs us of the chance to hear the truth of the gospel. If Jesus is not God the Son, then He is obviously no better or worse than Maitreya, who comes to 6,000 people in Africa with a few tricks up his sleeve and tells people that "salvation" is found in serving the people of this world by feeding them.

This is exactly what the Emergent Church is teaching. They have literally taken the true gospel off the table, replacing it with a social gospel that has no power to save but causes people to think that they are, in fact, working toward their salvation.

This is the biggest problem with false gospels. When all is said and done, these false gospels simply foist work on the backs of people. It is work for the sake of work. In authentic Christianity, we see a need and we try to meet it, always keeping in mind that the greatest need has to do with a person's soul; in other words, meeting that physical need becomes a means to the end, to introduce people to Jesus.

For those who follow a false gospel, the greatest need becomes the end. There is nothing beyond it.

My wife and I routinely carry business card-sized gospel tracts that we created and had printed up. Whenever we go out to eat, we make sure that we leave one of these cards. We also make sure that we leave a generous tip, because the tip shows our sincerity in recognizing how hard waiters/waitresses work for us while we are at that restaurant. To simply leave a card with no tip or a paltry tip is actually hypocritical. It is like saying "be warmed and fed!" and not helping in any way to accomplish that (cf. James 2:16). It has got to be difficult to be friendly and "up" for every customer served in a restaurant.

The Christian who does not try to meet the needs of people, but simply preaches to them, may wind up doing more harm than good. That's not to say that God's Word will return to Him void (it won't), but it is to say that Christians need to not only talk the talk, but we need to walk the walk.

False prophets/messiahs only walk the walk. People see what they do and they marvel. In the case of Maitreya, apart from feeding the hungry, he offers no truth at all, nothing of substance that actually saves people from their sin. He does nothing that brings them to the feet of Jesus. Maitreya simply re-introduces them to their Self, already on the throne. They feel good about feeding the hungry and begin to believe that the very act of feeding the hungry is the good work that provides them salvation. Nothing could be further from the truth.

What is key is not so much what we do in this life (action or work wise). What is key is who we know in this life. Of course, Jesus said it best in the judgment we know as the Sheep and the Goats.

In the last section of Matthew 25, we read of a judgment that is yet future. It actually occurs after the coming Tribulation. Jesus has just returned and set up His judgment seat as a preparatory measure for His millennial reign. As people are lined up before Him, they are placed into two groups: the sheep on the right and the goats on the left.

Here is the text from Matthew 25:31-46:

"But when the Son of Man comes in His glory, and all the angels with Him, then He will sit on His glorious throne. 32 All the nations will be gathered before Him; and He will separate them from one another, as the shepherd separates the sheep from the goats; 33and He will put the sheep on His right, and the goats on the left.

"34 Then the King will say to those on His right, 'Come, you who are blessed of My Father, inherit the kingdom prepared for you from the foundation of the world. 35 For I was hungry, and you gave Me something to eat; I was thirsty, and you gave Me something to drink; I was a stranger, and you invited Me in; 36 naked, and you clothed Me; I was sick, and you visited Me; I was in prison, and you came to Me.' 37 Then the righteous will answer Him, 'Lord, when did we see You hungry, and feed You, or thirsty, and give You something to drink? 38 And when did we see You a stranger, and invite You in, or naked, and clothe You? 39 When did we see You sick, or in prison, and come to You?' 40 The King will answer and say to them, 'Truly I say to you, to the extent that you did it to one of these brothers of Mine, even the least of them, you did it to Me.'

"41 Then He will also say to those on His left, 'Depart from Me, accursed ones, into the eternal fire which has been prepared for the

devil and his angels; 42 for I was hungry, and you gave Me nothing to eat; I was thirsty, and you gave Me nothing to drink; 43 I was a stranger, and you did not invite Me in; naked, and you did not clothe Me; sick, and in prison, and you did not visit Me.' 44 Then they themselves also will answer, 'Lord, when did we see You hungry, or thirsty, or a stranger, or naked, or sick, or in prison, and did not take care of You?' 45 Then He will answer them, 'Truly I say to you, to the extent that you did not do it to one of the least of these, you did not do it to Me.' 46 These will go away into eternal punishment, but the righteous into eternal life."

What is interesting here is that in most cases, the sheep were not even aware that they did things as if they were doing them to Jesus. They did not realize that by feeding people, giving them something to drink, visiting them in prison, etc., they were actually doing those things to Jesus.

Let's not lose sight of the truth, though. Jesus is not saying that these people earned salvation through these good works. It is very clear in another part of Matthew that just because people do the things listed above it does not mean they actually have salvation.

*"Not everyone who says to Me, 'Lord, Lord,' will enter the kingdom of heaven, but he who does the will of My Father who is in heaven will enter. 22 Many will say to Me on that day, 'Lord, Lord, did we not prophesy in Your name, and in Your name cast out demons, and in Your name perform many miracles?' 23 And then I will declare to them, '***I never knew you***; DEPART FROM ME, YOU WHO PRACTICE LAWLESSNESS."* (Matthew 7:21-23; emphasis added)

It would appear that the one requirement for entering into heaven to be with the Lord is that we know Him. It is clear that there are people who do many good works, but when all is said and done, they do not ultimately know the Lord at all. This means not only that they were never in relationship with Him, but He never knew them from before the foundations of the earth! Isn't that what He says? "I never knew you." There was never a time when they were in relationship with Jesus – ever. Their good works amounted to nothing as far as He was concerned because He was not in relationship with them.

So those people who are being taught and buy into the concept that doing things for others is all there is to it are sadly deceived. Yet they can actually become puffed up inside thinking of all the good they are doing throughout the world. They feel warm all over. They begin to be filled with a type of pride. Truly, they have their reward.

Look folks, it is becoming clear that deception is on the rise. Individuals like Maitreya will continue to appear, making claims and boasts that will seem to coincide with Jesus' teachings. In the end, they are so far from His teachings that we can honestly say their origin is in hell.

Maitreya showed himself to 6,000 people of Africa in 1988. He came neither with fanfare or heavenly sights. He came almost surreptitiously and incognito. The entire world did not see him. His arrival was secret, just as was his exit.

Jesus has clearly stated that when He returns, every eye will see Him. He has also stated that if you do not know Him by being in relationship with Him, you do not have salvation. Maitreya and others teach that salvation is gained through good works toward others. This is the very thing that separates Christianity from every other religion.

Jesus says you do not have to earn your salvation because He has made it available to you free of charge. False prophets/messiahs say that salvation must be earned.

Authentic Christians know that they must be involved in good works, not because those works save us, but because we are commanded to do them (cf. Ephesians 2:10). We understand that simply preaching the gospel of Jesus to people without caring for their needs normally does not amount to much because people are physical as well as spiritual. We meet the physical so that we can get their attention enough to meet the spiritual.

Maitreya says that we should meet people's physical needs – end of story. Jesus says that you should believe in who He is and what He has accomplished for you. I hope and pray that as you read this, you will ask yourself the one question that needs to be asked: what do you think of Jesus? Is He God the Son, or merely a good teacher with a heart of gold?

I pray that the Lord will open your eyes to the truth of who Jesus is and that you will embrace that truth. I pray that you will be able to say with Paul that "*if you confess with your mouth Jesus as Lord, and believe in your heart that God raised Him from the dead, you will be saved*" (Romans 10:9). Will you do that? Will you at least be willing to do that? God bless you as you contemplate the most important decision you will ever make in this life.

Chapter 19
Self in Society

I teach part-time at a local college, and as I was walking through the hall I saw one of the computer monitors on the wall. As usual, it was advertising something, in this case a relay run for the American Cancer Society. I didn't really pay attention to it.

After about the third time of walking past the monitor, the logo jumped out at me, and I remember thinking, *"What does that logo remind me of?"* As I looked at it, the light dawned. Well, I'll be doggone! Looks like the symbol that's on the Islamic flag! Could it be?

It looks like for this specific event, the individuals at the American Cancer Society added to their original logo what looks to be a slice of the moon (crescent) with the one star, in this case off to the left.

This leads to a question: did the folks at the American Cancer Society simply – by accident – come up with the new logo for the relay without intending to do so? That's kind of difficult to believe.

If they did not accidentally come up with it, then the only other answer is that they came up with it intentionally; however, they chose to make it *look* as though it was simply coincidental in nature. I don't buy it. I've been seeing the star and crescent too much in society as it is, and in fact, it seems to be permeating society on a global level.

So what do we make of this? Is it a conspiracy? Is it something that simply happens because the graphic artists all tend to think of crescent moons and a star? I think it's done intentionally to undergird people's thinking with things that are related to Islam. If this is correct, then that leads us to the question of why people (the movers and shakers) are doing this. What possible need does the world have to see the Islamic logo in everything?

Except for the fact that it sends hidden messages to radical Islamists, I'm not sure what other reason could possibly exist. But let's go off the deep end for a moment. If (and that's a fairly big "if") this is all part of the plan to indoctrinate the masses, what does it say to radical Islam?

I think it can only say one thing. It says, "We're with you. Go for it! Create chaos and we will look the other way!" If you stop to think about it, isn't that what is happening throughout the world now?

As I wrote about the other day in a blog I posted[21], the world is experiencing what many are calling "creeping Sharia." We are slowly seeing radical Islam encroaching upon various areas of society. In Dearborn, MI, with the most recent Arab Festival, non-Muslims were unceremoniously spit on. Though this assault was caught on video, no one was arrested.

In various parts of the world, Muslims are burning down Christian churches and gathering to demonstrate in protest of the fact that Jewish synagogues exist. This Muslim-on-Non-Muslim violence is getting out of hand, mainly because those in authority are complacent about it or simply do not want to do anything about it.

Can you imagine if one country was at war with another country – let's say country A and country B. What do you think would happen if country A attacked country B and country B essentially did nothing except back up and get out of the way? Their thinking would be, "If we leave them alone, they'll stop attacking us." If we saw a country do that, we would likely think of their leaders as morons. They are being attacked, yet instead of fighting back, they are simply giving in.

I believe that this is what is happening throughout the world. The problem, though, is that in our politically correct world, no one wants to say that the problem stems from one particular culture group. We don't mind a war against a country, but against one particular ethnicity or religious group? So, at every turn, our duplicitous leaders have chosen to walk around the problem, giving Islam a wide berth. Their thinking is that, like a ferocious barking dog, if you give it enough space, it will leave you alone.

Well, how much more do we have to see before our leaders will admit that being politically correct is a no-win situation for us? In

---

[21] http://www.studygrowknowblog.com

fact, being politically correct about the situation simply plays into the enemy's hands.

We have leaders in Washington who do not want anyone to say that we are at war with Islam. That's just not nice. It's counter-productive. Okay, then I will say it this way: Islam is at war with the world! To deny this is to deny our own rights and freedoms. It is giving up before we even pick up our weapons.

The more the world lies down, the more emboldened Islam will become. The more I study Islam, the more I see a complete lack of love and peace. I'm glad for those Muslims who are peaceful. They see the world through rose-colored glasses. If they truly believe that Islam is a "religion of peace," that's up to them, but when I read the Qur'an and watch the news, I see nothing that confirms that. In fact, Muhammad's own life negates the idea that love is the centerpiece of Islam.

So what do we do? Simple. We do not give in to their thugishness. We do not roll over and play dead. We also do not start acting like they are acting (though we want to). We do not go out of our way to imitate their behavior, but neither do we ask them "how high?" when they say "jump!"

I firmly believe that Islam is being used by the powers that exist in this world to create the type of catastrophic societal breakdown that will usher in the New World Order. It is really that simple. Once that happens, I believe these same "powers that be" will come down extremely hard on Islamic radicals to regain the order that was lost.

To us, it seems like an uncontrolled, volitional problem that is going to simply rise to the point of explosion. In fact, it is likely a very controlled, planned demolition of society that these world leaders believe is needed to usher in the next level of global change.

If we know that this is what is happening, we can at least be prepared for it. We don't have to succumb to the fear that drives the average person, and neither do we have to cave into the demands that we hear from the godless of this world.

The reality is that God is fully in control – always has been and always will be! There is nothing that slips by His notice.

I may be completely wrong about what I've said here today (except for the previous paragraph). Maybe the world powers have nothing to do with the rise of Islam. Maybe they are not trying to bring us to the brink of chaos so that they act the hero by setting up a New World Order. I don't believe that is the case. I go by what I see, and what I see in the world is telling me that something behind the scenes is catapulting this world to the brink of insane chaos. If you disagree with that, then I'm wondering if we are looking at the same world, and I do not mean that sarcastically.

Look at everything that has been happening since before Mr. Obama was elected. The tsunami of support that literally swept him into office (or so it seemed) changed the fate of this country.

Since taking the oath of office, Mr. Obama has seemingly worked diligently to do everything in his power to undercut the policies of our founding fathers. For example , in the case of the ICE (Immigration and Customs Enforcement), rather than work through Congress regarding illegal aliens into this country, the administration (though remaining in the background) has been working to change policy so that the hands of the individuals in the ICE are tied when it comes to determining who is and who is not here illegally.

Mr. Obama has defied Congress on several occasions (including the ongoing situation in Libya). He has been spending hand over fist the money from taxpayers of this nation. Tell me, with our economy as it is, why does the First Lady need to go to Spain or to Africa by herself?

We are experiencing food shortages throughout the world that are elevating prices at the grocery store. Gas prices continue to fluctuate. Flooding, earthquakes, tornadoes, and more are routine in the U.S., breaking records. Are these things happenstance, or are they being controlled? Is HAARP (High Frequency Active Aural Research Program) the common link? We know that it's capable of producing extremely high-quality images on the horizon as was recently done in China. Is it capable of creating heavenly signs and wonders as well?

This country is on the brink of financial destruction and our government seems unwilling or unable to do anything about it. Yesterday, during discussions of how to reduce the debt, many politicians simply walked out of the meeting led by VP Biden because they are fighting to keep new taxes off the table. The White House says it wants a "balanced approach" to debt reduction. Great, let's start with putting a moratorium on how much Mr. Obama can spend!

So what we are looking at the world over is tension that is often erupting in violence. Presently, Tunisia, Egypt, Sudan, Libya, Greece, and other areas of the world are experiencing social upheaval. Many countries are starting to crumble under the pressure of economic woes.

On top of that, we have Islamists demanding to have things done their way, and if that means that other people are denied their rights, too bad. This kind of upheaval in society causes the hearts of the people to fail them out of plain, old ordinary fear (cf. Luke 21:26). People are scared, and they have good reason to be. However, we were warned in Scripture that these days were coming. They are now here, and we have people who deny this reality.

Recently, Preterist Gary DeMar held a prophecy conference that derided those who still hold to a Premillennialist position, especially those of us who believe in a PreTrib Rapture. People like DeMar do not believe in the coming physical return of Jesus either, because they believe He returned in A.D. 70 when Rome crushed Jerusalem.

Yet when I look around, I see the words of Scripture coming to pass. I don't look at the newspaper and see where I can fit a specific event into the Bible. I look at the entire landscape and can clearly see that things that Jesus spoke of in the Olivet Discourse are now happening.

This is the problem, though, when you only look at one or two things. It takes the ability to see everything that is happening on the horizon. What is the overall picture?

I teach computer courses using Windows operating system and Microsoft Office. It is always interesting to me to see students who focus on the details, losing sight of the overall picture. Normally, each new chapter in the book teaches several skills for either Word, Excel, PowerPoint, or Access. It is easy to simply focus on this skill, which leads to that skill, which then leads to the next skill. What I try to do is help students understand what the project will look like when they are finished with it. The individual steps get them to the end. If they lose sight of the end and simply focus on each step as if that step is the end in and of itself, all they will become is thoroughly frustrated. Seeing the big picture helps them know that the steps are there for their use, not as an end in themselves.

I believe that God is fully and intimately involved in what is going on today. We can choose to focus on this or that as if those things will overcome us, or we can intelligently understand that the whole picture is designed by God, therefore He will give us the strength and wisdom to know how to react to the situation.

One thing is for sure. We are not to fear anything. There is absolutely nothing to fear. Do you fear Islam? You shouldn't. You should be willing to calmly stand against it. Do you fear running out of food? You shouldn't. You should take necessary measures to stock up on food and water and grow a garden if you can. If you fall prey to fear, you will be overtaken.

Instead, understand what is coming – and is already at the door – and make plans for yourself and your family. While God does not want us to fear, He also wants us to use His wisdom to know how we should prepare for these events.

Yes, these are dark days. However, I firmly believe that Christians have the best reason in the world to be filled with His joy, while overcoming the circumstances that are thrown in our paths. We worship the King of Kings and Lord of Lords! He will never leave or forsake us!

Islam is coming at us from all sides. Godless leaders are doing what they can to bring this country to its knees. Satan is doing everything he can to break into our world from his dimension in a more concerted effort than ever before. So? Our job is to be as gentle as doves and as wise as serpents (cf. Matthew 10:16). With that attitude, nothing can overcome us. We need to be aware of what is going on in our world. This is a must. We do not, however, need to fear any of it. God will supply the wisdom necessary to push through these problems with aplomb. God is GREAT!

God is still on the throne and, in fact, has never for one second been off of it! Authentic Christians need to start acting as if we believe it. Praise be to the God we serve!

Chapter 20
Self and Crime

Where do we begin with this subject? We all know about crime. Many of us have been victims of some type of crime, and it never feels good. You go to work, have a normal day there, and return home to find that your home has been broken into. You feel violated, and some of the things you worked hard to have are now gone. It is difficult to feel the same about your home after this because you know that someone came in and either damaged your property, took it, or both.

We have briefly touched on various types of crimes in this book in previous chapters, but I would like to spend some time detailing crime, not simply for the sake of it, but to point out one very important detail: *crime has roots that are deeply embedded in Self.*

That may appear obvious, but most of us do not think of that. In fact, the first question a person normally asks after a crime has been committed against them is, *why*? The crime may have been committed for any number of reasons, but ultimately, all of those reasons stem from some facet of Self.

We can think all the way back to Adam and Eve and the situation in which they were tempted to go against God's established order. What Satan did through the serpent, he did for purely selfish reasons. He was out to promote himself and destroy what God had created.

When Cain killed able, he did so because of the fact that Self (Cain's) was upset and jealous about the correct sacrifice that Abel had brought to God (cf. Genesis 4). Cain became indignant that his own sacrifice was not acceptable to God and his brother's was, so rather than acknowledge his mistake, Cain decides it was better to kill Abel. There, problem solved.

King David should have been out leading his troops in battle but instead chose to remain home in his palace. There, bored and lonely, he spied Bathsheba bathing on the roof of her home and lusted after her. His lust became adultery. Eventually, after it was determined that he had impregnated her, King David became a murderer by having her warrior husband, Uriah, placed in a section of the battle where he would be killed by the opposing soldiers (cf. 2 Samuel 11ff).

Why did King David do what he did? He did it because he began to listen to Self. Had Self come right out and said, "Hey, kill Uriah so you can be with Bathsheba!" David would have balked. So Self began to reel David in through what may have appeared relatively harmless:

lust. After all, he did not necessarily mean to see Bathsheba bathing. He was not deliberately being a peeping Tom. Instead of going back inside, he likely kept looking. Lust led to adultery, and to cover his sin, he became a murderer.

This all would not have occurred had David gone with his troops into battle, as he was supposed to have done. The second book of Samuel, chapter eleven, verse one tells us: *"Then it happened in the spring, at the time when kings go out to battle, that David sent Joab and his servants with him and all Israel, and they destroyed the sons of Ammon and besieged Rabbah.* **But David stayed at Jerusalem**" (emphasis added).

David chose to stay, in spite of the fact that this was the time when kings went out *with* their troops to battle. David said, *"Nah, I don't feel like it. Joab, you go in my place, all right?"*

The whole problem began because David chose to listen to Self. Self did not want to go into battle, so it caused David to feel as though he did not want to go, and David acquiesced. From there, David became bored, probably couldn't sleep – who knows, but maybe he was feeling guilty for not going with his troops – wandered out onto the palace roof, and there he saw Bathsheba. The rest, as we know, is history.

Giving into Self's demands created major problems for King David, his kingdom, and his family for generations. Self plays for keeps.

There is a great deal of criminal activity in our world today. Many lawmakers erroneously believe that by making more laws, the problem will be dealt with and crime will be reduced. This is simply not the case because criminals are not intimidated by the laws of the land as are law-abiding people.

Recently, large groups of mainly young men have taken to robbing – en masse – groups of people on buses, in stores, and elsewhere in parts of Illinois. Recently, in Peoria, groups of young black men were heard wandering through streets shouting that whites need to be exterminated. This is criminal, and they have obviously taken their cue from people like the ex-professor who stated as much.[22]

We have mentioned Islam a number of times throughout this book and with good reason. Radical Islam is not content unless it leads the way. It is not content to sit by and simply live by the status quo. It is important for radical Muslims to advance Islam any way they can achieve it. If that means using violence, they will use violence. If it means working within the system to find the loopholes, they will do that.

It does not help when our current administration turns a blind eye to the many problems that are created because of the existence of a culture of people who demand their way and will stop at nothing to gain the upper hand in society.

I really don't wish to harp on Islam, but the truth is that if we stop and look around the world, we will clearly see a great deal of criminal activity due to radical Muslims. However, for them, and because of what the Qur'an teaches, these things are not considered criminal. They are merely doing what they believe Muhammad teaches throughout the Qur'an.

It does not even matter to them that there are Muslims who claim to be moderate or peaceful. To these radicals, other Muslims are wrong, and they are not above killing them when push comes to shove, either.

Over the past few months, we have seen tremendous upheaval in parts of the Middle East because of the overthrow of specific governments. Due to the hole created by Egyptian dictator

---

[22] http://www.metacafe.com/watch/1543671/exterminate_white_people/ (06/27/2011)

Mubarak's downfall, the Muslim Brotherhood and other radical Islamic groups are doing all they can to fill in the gap and gain the majority voice in Egypt.

To that end, they are busy burning Christian churches and killing Christians. In other areas of the world, Muslims want to burn synagogues. Anything that is *not* Islam stands opposed to Islam and therefore must be eradicated.

This is the mentality of the radical Islamist, and it is contagious among groups who have felt disenfranchised. It is giving certain groups and individuals the strength to stand against those who seem to them to be standing in their way to achieve.

Islam is a huge threat to world peace because it will stop at nothing less than world domination. Radical Muslims believe this is their time to stand up and overcome the world. They believe that Allah is with them, and they ultimately believe they will be successful in achieving their goal of world domination. The only way they will not is if the rest of the world unites against Islam. These people are so blinded by Self that they are unable to see that what they are attempting to do is completely self-serving. They believe they can use any means necessary to push Islam's agenda on the world. Murder, rape, torture, theft – whatever – are simply means to the end goal. It is truly Self in all its glory. This is what Self does; it destroys utterly.

Yet much further down on the criminal scale we have the problem of homeless people. Let me state clearly that not all homeless people are criminal. Many today find themselves homeless because of the economy. They are victims of the problems created by banks and mortgage companies. They have lost their homes and are out on the streets. They have no other family they can turn to, so they turn to the state or charity organizations.

That is one type of homeless person. However, there is another type of homeless person who is homeless because they *want* to be homeless. Every time I take my wife to her work downtown, I see them.

There is a non-profit charity organization downtown that is so noted for its generosity that homeless people from other states actually find a way to come here so that their needs will be cared for and so they can continue to live as a homeless person! But what do homeless people do every day? It is not uncommon to see them walking along the sidewalk, pushing their grocery carts filled with all of their personal items.

They are unkempt, they sleep when they want, walk where they want, and essentially do whatever they want. They are homeless. They have no job, and many are not interested in obtaining a job even if one existed for them. They are content to be literally off the grid, living life as they please.

They beg for money, they root through the trash cans, and they wander. If they live near the organization downtown, they line up for breakfast and a shower, leave for a few hours, come back for lunch, leave for a few hours, come back for dinner, then leave to find a place to sleep.

If they get tired during the day (from all their walking), they plop themselves under a tree for a few hours of sleep, then get up and move along with the rest of their day. In essence, a person who wants to be homeless and continues to be homeless is the height of selfishness. They have no job, therefore they pay no taxes. They have their needs met and they simply wander. That is their life.

Now I realize – again – that there are many good people who are homeless because of the situation that has occurred in their life. These people are not interested in *remaining* homeless. They are busy looking for ways out of that life. The person who simply chooses the life of homelessness because it is easier for them is doing so because of Self's demands. These people do not care that they are deliberately draining society. All they care about is what they believe they need, and they have come to a point of entitlement that tells them repeatedly that the government owes them or that people on the street owe them, and they should pay up.

Self promotes disease. Whether it is selfishness or Self that prompts a criminal lifestyle, or a homeless lifestyle, the reality is that no good thing comes from Self. However, millions of people live for Self every day, in some form or another.

Self is something that people need to move away from, not embrace. Self will always demand more, and in the case of an authentic Christian, Self is still there, with the one difference (from the unsaved) that the Christian *can* and *should* overcome Self's desires and demands with the strength of the indwelling Holy Spirit.

I have to say that it chafes me a bit when people condemn me (or some other Christian) for messing up. It is as if they believe that Christians are to be perfect. Yet the illogical part is that they will admit that Christians are not perfect. No one is, and in fact, I know of no authentic Christian who actually teaches that Christians become perfect once they become Christians.

So on one hand, we have the world waiting for the authentic Christian to fail. When we fail, the world goes, "*Aha! You're a hypocrite!*" On the other hand, there is absolutely nothing in Scripture that promises I will become perfect in this life. If those in the world who stand opposed to Christianity would acknowledge what they know – that authentic Christians are not perfect – there would be less finger-pointing when we *do* fail.

It is no different from being pulled over by a police officer for speeding. Chances are good that the same police officer has broken the speed limit in his/her own personal car when not on duty. However, the person they have just pulled over broke the law right in front of the police officer, so they are being rewarded with a ticket.

Do we honestly believe that the same police officer writing the ticket has never broken the speed limit laws? We get annoyed because we were caught and now we are going to lose money. Our insurance rates may even rise.

If police officers were to be perfect, we would not have police officers at all. What we expect from our police officers is a general sense of decency toward the public and honesty in their work. It would be nice if they could be perfect, but no one can.

Authentic Christians are not perfect, and as far as I know we have never stated that we were or could be in this life. That is something that the world unfairly places upon us because they want every excuse possible to not have to become authentic believers themselves. This is Self.

Does the world actually believe that if a Christian makes a mistake, that lets them off the hook? I don't think so. Down deep, I believe they know the truth, but they prefer to believe what they want to believe because it makes their life easier for now.

I read of one guy on the 'Net who believed he found a foolproof way to show that Christians are hypocrites. His idea involved asking a Christian for $500 or $1,000. When the Christian would not provide it, the man would simply charge the Christian with hypocrisy.

Unfortunately for this man, his ridiculous challenge to Christianity amounts to nothing. He simply shows his lack of understanding where the Bible is concerned. He also fails to realize that there are many of us Christians who do not have an extra $500 or $1,000, and since we do not have it, we are not then hypocritical, but merely *poor*.

The world has all sorts of ways of denying the truth, because Self needs the truth denied. Self cannot handle the reality of the work of Jesus on the cross. Self cannot deal with the fact that we are not as important as we believe ourselves to be.

Self is the most destructive thing going today. It never stops creating havoc and because of that is extremely dangerous. If left unchecked, Self will destroy you. It cannot compete with God, so it makes itself a god. If you continue to listen to Self, you will only do those things that puff Self up, making it more important than it needs to be.

For this reason, Self should be ignored, but the average person cannot do that. The average person is in bondage to Self in one form or another. The only people who have half a chance of ignoring Self and submitting to God are those within whom the Holy Spirit dwells. "Apart from me, you can do nothing." Jesus said that in John 15:15 as He discussed the truth about the fact that He was/is the vine and we are merely the branches.

Those individuals who have submitted themselves to God, after realizing and then embracing the truth about who Jesus is and what He has accomplished for us, have the ability within them to overcome Self's demands. Without Him, we cannot accomplish it.

Your choice – should you decide to accept it – is to understand that you are nowhere near as great as you think you are and to also realize that we were not created to serve Self, but to serve God.

Chapter 21
Self in You

Do you know *when* you will die? Are you aware of the *day* and *hour* when you will slip from this life into eternity? I'm betting you are not privy to that information. So why are you living as if you **_do_** *know when it will happen?* Putting a decision about Jesus off until another day is taking a huge chance because of the fact that you do not know when you will die. That is plainly simple, and logic alone demands that you do not put this decision off. Yet you do, because the thought of becoming a Christian makes you feel uncomfortable.

You wrongly believe that to become a Christian means that you have to change in a major way *before* Jesus will accept you. It means to you giving up the things you love now because if you love them, then obviously they are wrong and God does not love them.

You are putting the cart before the horse. You must understand that God is not rejecting you. He is not standing there, tapping His foot, demanding that you eliminate those things that He does not like before you can come to Him for salvation.

If you (or anyone) could do that, you would not *need* His salvation at all. It is because you and I do things that are not pleasing to Him that we need His salvation.

What do you do that you would like to no longer do? Do you drink excessively until you cannot control it? Do you play around with drugs? Do you eat too much food until you have become overweight, lethargic and sickly?

What other things are in your life that you do not like? Are you drawn to illicit extra-marital affairs? Do you have a problem with lust? Are you a shopaholic? Do you tend to tell lies a great deal because it makes you feel important, or to hide things about your life?

Do you find that you do not like people and you would prefer to be around animals or out in the woods than around people? Are you a workaholic? Do you place a high value on money and you find that you work very hard to obtain it?

Here's the problem. The enemy of our souls comes to us and tells us that God will never accept us until we get rid of those things. He lies to us that God essentially wants us "perfect" before He will be willing to meet us and grant us eternal life. This is completely untrue.

The other lie that our enemy tells us is that we should not become a Christian because the fun in our life will fly out the door. We will no longer be able to drink or do the fun things we enjoy now. We start to think that coming to God means becoming a doormat for people and having to fill our life with things we do not want to *ever* do.

These are all lies, and unfortunately, too many people believe them. First of all, God does not expect you to be "perfect" before you come to Him for salvation. If that were the case, no one would be able to ever approach Him.

Secondly, God does not say that He is going to take away all the things we enjoy and replace them with things we hate. What is wrong with enjoying the lake on your boat? What is wrong with spending a day with the family fishing or just relaxing in the mountains? There is nothing wrong with these things.

What God *will* do is begin to remove the things that have ensnared you so that life is actually draining from you, but you are not aware of it. For instance, maybe you drink excessively and you have tried everything you can think of to quit. You have gone to AA meetings, spent thousands of dollars on this program or that, and you have even used your own will power to free yourself from the addiction to alcohol, all to no avail.

The question is not: *do I need to quit before I come to Jesus*? The question is: *am I willing to allow Him to work in and through me to take away the addiction I have to alcohol*? Do you see the difference? Are you willing to allow Him to work in you to break that addiction so that you will become a healthier person, one who is able to think straight and one who learns to rely on Him for strength? That is all He wants you to be able to do. He knows you cannot break that addiction (or any addiction for that matter) with your own strength and willpower. Are you willing to allow Him to do it in and through you?

What if you are a workaholic? What if you have "things" like a boat, a house in Cancun, a large bank account, four cars, and more? Do you think that God is going to ask you to give it up, or worse, do you think that God will simply come in and take all of that from you? I know of nothing in Scripture that tells us He will do that.

What God will do with all of those who come to Him trusting Him for salvation is one thing, which begins the moment we receive salvation and will continue until the day we stand before Him. He will begin to create within us the character of Jesus (cf. Ephesians 2:10).

Here is a verse from the Old Testament that was said originally through the prophet Ezekiel to the people of Israel. While this was specifically stated to the Jews, it is applicable to all who receive salvation through Jesus Christ.

"I will give you a new heart and put a new spirit within you; I will take the heart of stone out of your flesh and give you a heart of flesh. I will put My Spirit within you and cause you to walk in My statutes, and you will keep My judgments and do them" (Ezekiel 36:26-27).

God is speaking here through Ezekiel, and He is saying that He will give the people a new heart of flesh, removing that old heart of stone. This is God's responsibility. God is the One who makes that happen. We are told in the book of Hebrews that God is the Author and Finisher of our faith (cf. Hebrews 12:2). This tells me that God is the One who changes me from within so that over time, my desires are slowly turned into His desires.

I recall years ago thinking that God wanted to do everything in my life that I did not want Him to do. I fell into the asinine belief that He wanted to change everything about me. What I learned is that yes, there are things that God does want to change about me. However, there is a lot that God originally gave me that He has also enhanced and used for His glory.

Maybe you are a workaholic who thinks that working hard is something God does not want you to do. This is not necessarily the case. He may have given you the ability and the knowledge to work in the area of finance for a great purpose. All He may wind up doing is dialing back your workaholic tendencies so that you have more time to enjoy your family and study His Word.

But you say you smoke, or drink, or use illegal drugs, and you don't want to give those up. As I stated, you can't give those up under your own power, and the fact that you have tried so many times has proven it to you.

But God knows what is and what is not good for you. Are you willing to *allow* Him to work in you to change your desires so that you no longer want to smoke, use illegal drugs, or drink nearly as much?

Then you say that you believe God wants to make you a Christian so you can become miserable. Isn't that what most Christians are – miserable? Not the Christians I know, and certainly not me, my wife, or our children.

Where does the Bible say that God wants us miserable? You will not find it. What God wants is for us to be blessed, and that begins when we receive salvation from His hand.

You know, if we would stop and take the time to consider the fact that this life is exceedingly short if we compare it to eternity, we will then realize that there is nothing so important that it should keep us from receiving Jesus as Savior and Lord.

Unfortunately, too many people do not consider the brevity of life. They think they will live forever, or at the very least, they will die when they are really old and gray. That will come too soon. Even though I have just recently turned 54, it still truly seems like yesterday that I was a young boy fishing in the Delaware River near Hobart, New York. There I spent many Saturdays fishing and simply enjoying being outdoors. How did life go by so very quickly? How could that have happened?

It has happened, and I am at a point in life where not only do I realize that this life is short, but I actually look forward to spending eternity with Jesus after this life. Does that sound morbid to you? It shouldn't, because by comparing this life to eternity, we should get a sense of what is truly important.

God does not expect us to become Mother Theresas. He does not necessarily expect us to give up everything and become missionaries in outer Mongolia. What God expects is for us to simply allow Him to change our character as He sees fit.

Over time, we may well find that we have simply stopped swearing without realizing it. Our desire for cigarettes or alcohol has nearly evaporated. Illicit affairs no longer enter the picture.

We also may find that some of the things we want to eliminate in our life become more pronounced. Often the enemy will do this to cause us to focus on something that God is not even doing in our lives at that point. It causes tension, frustration, and self-anger.

If you have gotten to this point in your life and you have not dealt with the question about Jesus, it is about time you do so. You need to stop what you are doing and realize a couple of things before you go through another minute in this life.

- **Sinner**: you need to realize that you are a sinner. You have sinned and you will continue to sin. Sin is breaking the laws that God has set up. We all sin. We have all broken God's laws and that breaks any connection we might have had with God. Sin pushes us away from Him.

    Romans 3:23 says, *"For all have sinned, and come short of the glory of God."* That means you and that means me. All means all. That is the first step. We need to recognize and agree with God that yes, we are sinners. I'm a sinner. You are a sinner. This results in God's anger, what the Bible terms "wrath."

- **God's Wrath**: Romans 1:18 says, *"For the wrath of God is revealed from heaven against all ungodliness and unrighteousness of men, who suppress the truth in unrighteousness."*

This is as much a fact as the truth that we are all sinners. Because we are sinners – by breaking God's law(s) – God has every right to be angry with us and ultimately destroy that which is sinful. If we choose to remain "in" our sinful states throughout this life, we will – unfortunately – be destroyed with the rest of sin.

Fortunately, there *is* a remedy, and it is salvation.

- **God's Gift**: In the sixteenth chapter of Acts, a jailer asks Paul this famous question: *what must I do to be saved?* The question was asked because Paul and Barnabas had been imprisoned, and while there, they began singing praises to God.

God then sent a powerful earthquake that opened the doors to all the prison cells, yet no one escaped. When the jailer arrived, he saw that everyone was still in their cells, and after seeing that miracle (what prisoner would not want to escape from prison?), turned and asked what he must do to be saved. He was speaking of the spiritual aspect of things. He wanted to know how he could be guaranteed eternal life.

The answer Paul gave the man was, *"Believe on the Lord Jesus Christ, and thou shalt be saved, and thy house"* (Acts 16:31).

This is not head knowledge or intellectual assent. This is *believing from the heart.* In fact, Paul makes a very similar statement in another book he wrote, Romans. He says, *"That if thou shalt confess with thy mouth the Lord Jesus, and shalt believe in thine heart that God hath raised him from the dead, thou shalt be saved. For with the heart man believeth unto righteousness; and with the mouth confession is made unto salvation"* (Romans 10:9-10).

When we fully believe something, we confess that it is true. It must begin in the heart because that is where the will is located. We must want to believe. We must endeavor to believe. We must seek to believe.

We must stop giving ourselves all the reasons to deny or ignore Jesus. As God, He became a Man, born of a virgin. He clothed Himself with humanity that He might show us how to live, and in so doing, would keep every portion of the law.

If Jesus was capable of keeping every portion of the law, then He would be found worthy to become a sacrifice for our sin – yours and mine. If He became a sacrifice for our sin, then all that we must do is embrace Him and His sacrificial death.

In short then, to become saved we must:

1. Admit (we sin)
2. Repent (want to turn away from it)
3. Believe (that Jesus is the answer)
4. Embrace (the truth about Jesus)

We **admit** that we are sinner, that we have sinned. This is nothing more than agreeing with God that we have broken His law. Can you honestly say that you have not broken God's law? If you admit to breaking even the "smallest" law, then you are a lawbreaker.

After we admit that we have sinned, the next step is found in **repenting**. Some believe that repenting is actually moving away from sin. This author believes that it is a willingness to move away from sin, and there is a difference.

As we have already discussed, it is impossible to stop sinning. Human beings simply cannot do it because as long as we live, we will have a sin nature, which is something within us that gives us a propensity to sin. As long as we have this inner propensity to sin or break God's laws, we will never be perfect in this life.

We cannot one day say, "Lord, I promise to stop sinning." If we do that, we are only kidding ourselves and setting ourselves up for major failure. We cannot stop sinning in this life. The most we can do is *want* to stop sinning and then spend the rest of our lives allowing God to create the character of Jesus within us, slowly, little by little.

Repenting is to decide that you no longer want to do the things that keep us out of heaven. We no longer wish to break God's laws. It is not promising God that we will never sin again.

Once we admit, then repent, we must **believe**. This is one of the most difficult things to do because believing that Jesus died in our place, that He lived a perfectly sinless life, is extremely difficult to believe. Our minds cannot grasp that truth. We must ask God to open our eyes to that truth so that we can embrace it.

While on the cross next to Jesus, the one thief joined the other thief in ridiculing Jesus. Then, all of a sudden – as we read in Luke 23 – this same thief that had just been ridiculing Him now turned to Him with a new understanding.

It was this new understanding that prompted the thief to say to Jesus, "*Lord, remember me when you come into your Kingdom.*" Jesus looked at the man and responded to him, "*Today, you will be with me in paradise.*"

What had occurred in the mind and heart of that thief from one moment to the next? One thing, and that one thing was that God opened the thief's eyes so that he could see the truth. It was as if the blinders fell off and he now saw and understood who Jesus was, even to the most cursory degree that Jesus was dying not for Himself, but for others.

It was this understanding, this awareness, which prompted the man to ask Jesus to simply be remembered. Jesus went way beyond it to promise the man that he would be with Jesus that day in paradise.

Please notice in Luke 23 that there is nothing in the chapter that tells us that the man promised Jesus he would give up sin, or that he would never sin again. There is nothing that tells us that thief took the time to enter into a final deathbed confession of his sins so that he could be absolved.

The thief made no promises to Jesus at all. What he experienced was the truth of who Jesus was and what Jesus accomplished for humanity. Jesus accomplished what we cannot. What is left is for each person to *admit, repent, believe,* and *embrace*.

Let me clarify here that though we do not see any verbal repentance from the thief, we know that he did repent. He admitted as well. How can we know this? Simply due to the thief's complete about-face with respect to his attitude toward Jesus. One minute, he was ridiculing Jesus, and the next, embracing Him. This is important.

There is no way he could have or would have *embraced* Jesus had he not been humbled by the truth *about* Jesus.

Once the thief saw the truth, he was instantly humbled. Within himself, he knew that he was a sinner, and in fact the text states that this is what he told the other thief dying next to him. *"But the other answering rebuked him, saying, Dost not thou fear God, seeing thou art in the same condemnation? And we indeed justly; for we receive the due reward of our deeds: but this man hath done nothing amiss"* (Luke 23:40-41). Something happened within the heart of the one thief. In one moment, the thief went from harassing Jesus to recognizing his own sinfulness and then ultimately asking for grace, which was freely given to him.

Whether he said it or not, the thief went from haughtiness to humility in a very short space of time, and it was all because he saw the truth about Jesus. That truth helped him realize that he deserved his death and what would happen to him after death. He understood that Jesus did not deserve death.

From here, the thief fully embraced the truth about Jesus and was rewarded with eternal life because of it. He did not come off the cross to be water baptized. He did not list a long litany of offenses against God. He recognized the truth about Jesus, was humbled, and embraced that truth!

This is what each of us needs to do. We cannot give in to the lie that tells us that we are not good enough, or we have not given up enough before God will accept us. We must reject the lie that says we must somehow earn our salvation.

Jesus has done everything that is necessary to make salvation available to us. The only thing that is left for us is to see the truth. Once we see that truth, it should humble us to the point of embracing Jesus and all that He stands for and is to us.

The eighth chapter of Romans begins with the fact that all who trust Jesus for salvation are no longer condemned...*ever*. All of my sins – past, present, and future – have not only been forgiven, but canceled. It is because of my faith in the atonement (death) of Jesus that God is able to cancel all of my sins, even the ones that I have not committed yet. This does not make me eager to commit them. It makes me want to do what I can to avoid sinning.

If you do not know Jesus, please do not put down this book without deliberately *believing* that He is God, that He died for you by the shedding of His blood on the cross, and that He rose three days later because death could not keep Him. Do you believe that? If you do not yet believe it, do you *want* to believe it? If so, then simply ask God to help you come to believe all that Jesus is and all that He has accomplished for you. God will answer your prayers and you may either receive instantaneous awareness of all that Jesus is and has done, or it may be a *growing* awareness over time. In either case, it is the most important decision you will ever make.

Turn to Him now and pray for knowledge of the truth and an ability to embrace it. Please. He is waiting for you.

Ask Yourself:

1. Do you *know* Jesus? Are you in *relationship* with Him? Have you had a spiritual transaction according to John 3?
2. Do you *want* to receive eternal life through the only salvation that is available?
3. Do you believe that Jesus is God the Son, who was born of a virgin, lived a sinless life, died a bloody and gruesome death to pay for your sin, was buried, and rose again on the third day? Do you *believe* this?
4. Do you *want* to *embrace* the truth from #3?
5. Pray that God will open your eyes and provide you with the faith to begin believing the truth about Jesus. Ask Him to help your faith embrace the truth, realizing that you are not good enough to save

yourself and that your sin will keep you out of God's Kingdom without His salvation.

6. Pray as if your life depended upon it because *it does*!
7. If you have prayed to receive Jesus as Savior and Lord, please write to me. I want to send you some materials at *no charge or obligation*. Write to me at **fred_deruvo@hotmail.com** and sign up for our free bimonthly newsletter at **www.studygrowknow.com**

Visit our page on **OnePlace.com/ministries/study-grow-know** to hear our latest broadcasts as well as those that have been archived.

SELF

ALIENology is somewhat of a science for many who believe that entities from other planets or dimensions enter and leave our dimensions at will. What can we learn from these beings? Anything truthful? Dr. Fred believes that putting our faith in anything these beings say may be a huge leap in the wrong direction. Aliens reportedly come in all shapes, sizes, and even cultural representations. Because of this, there tends to be a good deal of mixed messages out there, yet people believe it because of their experience. Anything wrong with that picture? ($14.99; 176 pages, 978-0983700609)

Raised for His Glory delves into the books of Ezekiel and Romans to determine what the Bible actually says about Israel. Is the section on Ezekiel 36-39 speaking of a future time when nations will gather against Israel, or is this something that has already occurred? Moreover, just exactly what is the Valley of the Dry Bones referring to – the nation of Israel, or the Church? Join Dr. Fred as he presents his understanding of these very important sections of God's Word and how they relate to the only nation that He ever created, *Israel*. ($15.99; 190 pages, 978-0983700623)

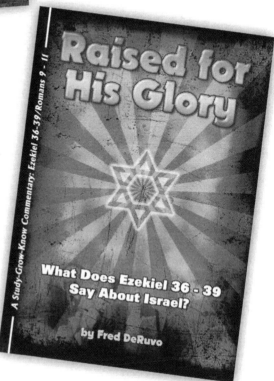

There is a chaos coming that is predicated upon the rise of Islam, Satanic Soldiers, aliens, and evil beyond measure. As an ideology, Islam masquerades as a religious light to the world, one that promises to usher in world peace – but at what cost? Through the use of political strategies, military might, and religious tenets, adherents of Islam work within various established governments to create special laws or exemptions for Muslims in the hope of eventually overthrowing that established government. Can it happen? IS it happening? Find out in *Evil Rising*. ($13.95; 184 pages, 978-0977424429)

We hear all the time how bad things are getting throughout the world. Do we chalk it all up to being the normal cycles that occur in life, or is something else going on behind the scenes? What if this generation alive now turns out to be the last one before Jesus returns? Is there any truth at all to the claim that Jesus will return one day? If you are one who has not taken the time to read through some of the books of the Bible that are said to teach truths regarding the last days, *Living in the Last Generation* puts it out there in a straightforward manner, making it easy to understand. ($11.95; 132 pages, ISBN: 978-0977424405)

Made in the USA
Charleston, SC
24 October 2011